5/10

Paul G. Bahn, M.A., Ph.D., F.S.A., is a freelance archaeologist based in Hull, who has written, edited and translated numerous books on a wide variety of aspects of archaeology.

His main specialities are prehistoric art, especially Ice Age art, and Easter Island. He is a guide-lecturer on tours to the European Ice Age decorated caves and to Easter Island every year.

This is his first non-archaeological book.

The Cambridge Rapist:
Unmasking The Beast Of Bedsitland

For Y

Paul G. Bahn

The Cambridge Rapist:
Unmasking The Beast Of Bedsitland

Vanguard Press

VANGUARD PAPERBACK

© Copyright 2012
Paul G. Bahn

A CIP catalogue record for this title is
available from the British Library.

ISBN 978 1 84386 851 4

*Vanguard Press is an imprint of
Pegasus Elliot MacKenzie Publishers Ltd.*
www.pegasuspublishers.com

First Published in 2012

**Vanguard Press
Sheraton House   Castle Park
Cambridge   England**

Printed & Bound in Great Britain

Picture Acknowledgements

For supplying pictures, I am most grateful to Gill Hughes (Museum Lead, Cambridgeshire Constabulary).

The pictures on p.122 are reproduced by kind permission of PRIVATE EYE magazine www.private-eye.co.uk.

Photographs were also acquired from the *Cambridge Evening News*, and from News International Syndication (photos by Tony Eyles, *The Sun*)

Some photos of the period now seem to be unavailable from any source, and so had to be scanned from the original articles, by kind permission of the *Cambridge Evening News*.

My thanks also go to Mercy Kaggwa and all at Pegasus for preparing this book for publication.

Contents

Introduction

During one grimly memorable academic year, from October 1974 to June 1975, the city of Cambridge was gripped by fear, as one man carried out a series of rape attacks which steadily grew in violence and caused widespread terror. There have been few other examples anywhere in the world of one criminal laying siege to an entire city and causing many of its inhabitants to tighten their security and lose sleep through sheer terror.

I was a graduate student at Cambridge University at that time. My subject was archaeology, and one of its many aspects which attracted me was that it was a kind of detective work. As a youth I had devoured the Sherlock Holmes stories, admiring his deductive process of thought, and had at one point entertained thoughts of becoming a detective myself. For some reason, I developed a particular interest in serial crimes, such as those of Jack the Ripper or the Moors Murderers; and so, as soon as the Cambridge rapist's second attack made it seem likely that this was turning into a series of similar incidents, I began to follow the story closely, poring over every detail in the local newspaper articles devoted to it.

Ironically, it was this interest which led me to have my room searched by the police and to be interrogated myself (see chapter 7). Later I was also involved on the margins of these tragic events as a member, and later organiser, of the unique student bodyguard service (chapter 10).

Once the rapist was caught and imprisoned, I assumed that books would soon emerge on this extraordinary case. In particular I felt sure that Fulton Gillespie, the journalist on the *Cambridge Evening News* who had written almost all of the relevant articles and who had done all the background research, would produce the definitive account of events. But to my great surprise, nothing appeared. In the early 1980s I contacted Mr Gillespie, as I had begun to have thoughts of writing my own account. He informed me that he had indeed produced a manuscript on the Cambridge rapist, but that he had not found a publisher — in part because a general book on women and rape (*Against our Will: Men, Women and Rape* by Susan Brownmiller) had appeared in 1975, and in part because of a less-than-efficient agent.

I therefore shelved my idea, assuming once again that the Gillespie manuscript would eventually be published, since it existed. But it has never seen the light of day; and, even more amazingly, not a single book has ever been published on this unique and astonishing episode in a great university city. So I have decided to put one together myself. The rapist is long dead, and Fulton Gillespie lives in retirement outside Cambridge, and most of the others involved — such as the police investigators — are likewise retired or deceased. The rapist's unfortunate young victims are probably mothers or even grandmothers after all these years. One can only hope that the passing of time had a healing effect and that they eventually were able to come to terms with their traumatic ordeals. I fervently hope that this book will not cause any of them any distress, even though it will inevitably arouse some terrible memories, and I was determined from the start to protect their anonymity.

It goes without saying that much of my account is heavily reliant on the investigative reporting of Fulton Gillespie, and I am profoundly grateful to him for giving my project his blessing. Special thanks are also owed to ex-DS Bernard Hotson, one of the leaders of the manhunt, and ex-DC Terry Edwards, who caught and arrested the Rapist, for having the kindness and patience to answer my questions; to Sam Clift and Bob Wordsworth for assistance with police matters; and to my old friend James Monnington who sent me his recollections of his "close encounter" with that evil little man.

As I was finishing the manuscript, in a bizarre twist of fate another hooded cyclist with good local knowledge was making sex attacks in Cambridge; he had begun in August 2010, and by June 1st 2011 had assaulted nine young females, all but one of them students. He would clasp a gloved hand over their mouth from behind, and then grope them through their clothing; when they struggled or screamed, he ran off. Police have warned girls not to walk alone at night, and a £5000 reward has been offered for information leading to an arrest. Although his activities are doubtless a traumatic experience for the victims and a frightening prospect for all girls in Cambridge, it has to be said that this is a minor serial crime when compared with the atrocities perpetrated by Cook. Let us hope that the new attacker will soon be caught, and that Cambridge will never again experience anything like the Rapist's reign of terror.

Paul G. Bahn, June 2011

Chapter 1
The first attack

In October 1974, life for a student in Cambridge was the usual mixture of work and fun, or fun and work, depending on one's priorities. Outside the endless round of lectures and supervisions, of work-sessions in libraries and various college activities, many students crowded into their college TV rooms every week to watch *Top of the Pops*, with bands like Mud, Status Quo and the Bay City Rollers riding high at that time. There were also films to be seen such as *Chinatown* or *Blazing Saddles*, star-studded debates to attend at the Union Society, and plays and revues to enjoy: the annual Footlights Christmas pantomime at the end of that year, *Babes in the Wood*, was directed by Griff Rhys Jones and featured a long-haired Clive Anderson. Actually, many of us, myself included, had shoulder-length hair at that time, as well as unspeakably awful flowery shirts and bell-bottom trousers. Those years definitely deserved their reputation as the decade that taste forgot.

The medieval centre of Cambridge, including my own college, Gonville and Caius, is a haven, a peaceful core with a more bustling and modern city around it. During term-time it is still filled with cyclists rather than motorists. By 1974 the stringent rules of earlier decades — such as can be seen in the 1958 film *Bachelor of Hearts* — had been relaxed. Students no longer had to wear gowns, let alone mortar boards, outside their college, and they could stay out far into the night, and enter their colleges very late, without having to attempt to scale the high walls and spikes to regain entry (often in a state of some inebriation), while avoiding being detected and caught by the "bulldogs", the university's rule-enforcers.

One aspect, however, had not yet advanced very far: for decades there had only been three colleges for female undergraduates (Girton, Newnham, New Hall) but more than twenty male colleges. In 1972, three male colleges — King's, Churchill and Clare — had become mixed-sex establishments. Nowadays, almost all the colleges are mixed, with only a few remaining single-sex: in the 2004/5 academic year, 52% of students were male and 48% female. But thirty years earlier there was still a tremendous imbalance between the numbers of male and female students, which inevitably caused enormous frustrations on the male side.

There were around 13,000 students. A great number of them lived in rooms in their colleges; but many others lived in bedsits outside the colleges, often in houses belonging to the different colleges, which own a great deal of property. Consequently, there were many houses in the city of Cambridge which were entirely occupied by young female students, and of course there were also many others occupied by young women who were not students but "civilians".

Cambridge had never really been known for crime; life there was generally peaceful, and its newspaper, the *Cambridge Evening News*, was a typical provincial publication, filled with regional stories, local events and misdemeanours. All that was about to change.

On Saturday October 19th, shortly after the start of the Michaelmas term, a small paragraph appeared at the bottom of the newspaper's front page. It read as follows:

Girl raped in flat

A 20-year-old single girl was raped at home in her flat in the Mitcham's Corner area of Cambridge last night between 9 and 10 p.m., police said today. Her attacker, a young man in his mid-20s, dressed in casual clothing, also stole a small amount of cash from the flat.

Cambridge police are anxious to speak to anyone who was in the Mitcham's Corner area at that time last night. They were carrying out intensive enquiries in the area today.

No further details emerged at that time, but it was later learned what had happened to the girl, Frances A, a secretary new to the city. According to her statement: "My room is on the first floor of the house in Springfield Road which I rent together with two other girls. We each have a bedroom of our own, and on the ground floor are the kitchen and bathroom, which we share. One of the girls has a boyfriend staying at the moment, and they had all gone to a football match [that night]... so I was alone at home. I settled down to cooking, and ate while watching TV. Afterwards I washed up and, when I'd finished, I went to my car and fetched a bag. The car was parked in a sidestreet at the side of the house, and it took me a few minutes at most. I left the door unlocked while I was fetching the bag. But I didn't see anyone go in the house.

I then sat down again and watched TV. At 8.30 I watched the start of 'No Honestly'. Then I went upstairs. That must have been shortly after 8.30, as the programme 'No Honestly' began at that time. I unpacked my bag. Then I went to the bathroom on the ground floor. After the bath I again went up to my room, where I put a knitted shawl round myself. I didn't have anything else on. I went down again with my transistor radio, which I switched on while I washed my hair. Then I put my dressing gown on, and went out into the kitchen to make sure that the back door of the house was locked. I went back to my room, closed the door and left the hall lights on. I switched on the light in my room and turned on the TV set which stood in front of my bed. The bed was opposite the door, on the right.

I never locked my room door. But it was fitted with a Yale lock, and there was a key at the outer side. I sat on my bed and watched the 'Morecambe and Wise' show on TV. When it finished, I switched off and began to dry my hair. I set up my cassette recorder, and certainly a quarter of an hour went past. When my hair was dry I turned off the hair dryer. I guess the time was 9.20.

Suddenly the light in my room went out. It became totally dark. I don't think the time was more than 9.30; and then I heard a sound from outside.

I began to get really nervous. I put on the shawl and opened the door. 'Is anyone there?' I asked. There was no answer. I closed the door quickly and began to rummage in my drawers and cupboard for a candle. As I stood and rummaged in the cupboard I had my back to the door. Suddenly I heard someone turning the key in the lock!

I ran to the door to keep it closed. I can't remember exactly what happened. But I felt someone on the other side, and this 'someone' was pushing, and it became an exhausting struggle. I used all my strength to stop him, but I suppose it was only a matter of seconds before he got the door open.

I fell back to the bed as he carefully pushed the door-bolt up. Then he came in and pushed me to the floor. He had a scarf in front of the lower part of his face. I screamed when he came in. And I remember he told me to be quiet and, if I did exactly as he said, he'd do me no harm. He lay or stood on me, held me tightly to the floor. I couldn't move.

'I've got a very sharp knife with me and one silly move and there will be a lot of blood.' He asked, 'Have you got anything I can tie your hands with?' I said, 'I don't know.' My chest of drawers stood just at his side, and he used one hand to hurriedly rummage through the drawers, while he held me with the other. Then he took out a blouse and used it to tie my hands behind my back. He tightened it hard and asked, 'Is that tight enough?'

He rummaged round in my chest of drawers and my cupboard, and I tried to sit up. I didn't see the knife but I was so frightened of it that I daren't scream. My dressing gown had come undone as it's only got a tie belt. I struggled to cover myself up but I couldn't with my hands tied. When he saw what I was thinking, he came and pushed me down to the bed. I lay on my back on the bed and I was face to face with him, but I couldn't see him!

He quickly got a pillowcase off and put it over my head, leaving me just enough room to breathe. 'I came to rob you but I think I'll rape you first.' He tumbled onto the bed with me, lifted my dressing gown up, and I was now really scared. I kicked out at him, so he grabbed my legs. He held my legs up in the air. I couldn't see him unbutton his trousers, but as he leaned over me between my legs I could feel his penis on my skin. I think his trousers were fastened with a zip. I can't remember what his clothes looked like.

He put his penis up me. I can't remember if he used anything — a rubber or suchlike. I was paralysed. I couldn't scream. While he was raping me, he said, 'Are you enjoying it?' I couldn't say anything, I was filled with fear and shock. When he'd finished he got out of me. He pushed me hard under the blanket and pulled a pillowcase down over my head. My hands were still tied. I could hardly breathe, but he took no notice until he stuck his hands under the blanket and pretended to strangle me. I was terrified, he was so rough.

'Don't try to get loose', he snarled. 'I can't breathe', I said, 'won't you take the pillowcase off?' He did that. Then he went into one of the other girls' rooms and fetched a blanket which he laid over me. I was pleased. I saw my legs were free.

'Have you anything I can take?', he said. 'Money?' He came and pressed my head down into the pillow and repeated that he had a knife and there'd be lots of blood if I didn't tell him where he could find money. I told him the money was in a leather pouch in the bag. There was a £5 note and the rest was in £1 notes, £12 in all. He looked round the room for something else. He found my jewellery and took something from it.

When he went, I could hear him going round the other girls' rooms and rummaging. He bumped into a dressing-table. A bit later I heard him go downstairs. The next thing that happened was that music came from my cassette recorder again, at the same time as the light went on in the room.

I don't know how long I lay there but it must have been fifteen minutes before I grabbed my trousers and drove to friends a mile and a half across town. He was about twenty years old, 5 ft 4 ins., medium build with light brown hair just below his ears. Because he had some covering over the lower part of his face, his voice was muffled. He wore medium blue denim jeans. I was a virgin. I had never had sexual intercourse with anyone before this happened. I can remember that after he'd put his penis up, he also tried to put it in my bottom. When he had no luck with that, he stuck it in my vagina again, and brought himself off. I was so shaken by everything I can't really remember my reaction. But it hurt. Unfortunately I don't think I'd know him again."

Frances' testimony was important because it revealed that her rapist was only 5 ft 4 ins. However, due to the darkness, she was utterly mistaken about his age, an error which was to have terrible repercussions for every young man in Cambridge of less than average height.

****

One can readily understand that hardly anyone paid much attention to the tiny newspaper article of October 19th. A rape was a rare event in Cambridge, and obviously a tragic and deeply unpleasant act, but there seemed no reason to attach any great significance to this particular case. Alarm bells started ringing, however, when a second, very similar attack occurred exactly two weeks later — once again on a Friday night, and at a similar hour.

Girl raped in flat

A 20-year-old single girl was raped at home in her flat in the Mitcham's Corner area of Cambridge last night between 9 and 10 p.m., police said today.

Her attacker, a young man in his mid-20's, dressed in casual clothing, also stole a small amount of cash from the flat.

Cambridge police are anxious to speak to anyone who was in the Mitcham's Corner area at that time last night. They were carrying out intensive enquiries in the area today.

First article published in *The Cambridge Evening News*, Saturday 19th October 1974

Chapter 2
The second attack

ALERT AFTER
SECOND CITY
SEX ATTACK

On Saturday November 2nd, the *Cambridge Evening News* carried some chilling news. The article was still quite short, but it was beneath a big headline:

ALERT AFTER SECOND CITY SEX ATTACK

Cambridge police today warned all women alone in their homes to keep their doors and windows locked after the second sexual assault on a young girl within two weeks. A 20-year-old girl alone in her bed-sitter in the Elizabeth Way area of Cambridge was assaulted last night between 9 p.m. and 9.30 p.m. The police said the circumstances were similar to the rape of another girl alone in her flat in the Mitcham's Corner area of Cambridge on October 18, also a

> Friday night. That offence took place between 9 and 10 p.m.
>
> They were almost certain that the same man was responsible for both offences. The spokesman said that the police were very concerned and making intensive door-to-door inquiries. Tracker dogs were used in the hunt for the attacker last night after the girl ran to a neighbour's home to call for help.
>
> "We appeal for anyone who might have seen anything suspicious last night at that time near Elizabeth Way to contact Cambridge police immediately", he said. Police believe the attacker may be a man with a good knowledge of Cambridge's bed-sitter land and what goes on in the area.

How right they were! However, no further details of the second attack were divulged at that time, not even the information they already had on the rapist's height and apparent age, details which had been more-or-less confirmed by the second victim.

The girl's name was Anne B. She had been in Cambridge for over three years, had a regular boyfriend and was planning to marry. Her ordeal in the flat in Abbey Road bore some striking similarities to that of Frances:

"It was about 8.30 on Friday evening. I was in the bath listening to "Any Questions" on the radio, when I thought I heard someone in the house. I can remember that before I went upstairs I'd locked the outer door. There's a Yale lock in the door; but I couldn't remember having locked the back door.

Twenty minutes after I'd heard a noise in the house, the bathroom light went out. I thought the fuse had blown, so I wanted to go out to the meter. I got out of the bath, slipped on a vest, went out on the landing, went to the meter and tried the contacts — it didn't work. But there was obviously no one to help me. I tried the light switch which also didn't work. I put on an old dressing gown, went back onto the landing, leaned over the banister and I could see someone standing in the doorway of the breakfast room. I said, 'Is that you?' The man said, 'Yes'.

I could see his outline. He had shoulder-length hair which was similar to that of someone I know but he was not big enough. My friend is big and plump. I called again, and the bloke started to come up the stairs. I was still standing on the landing at the top. When he'd come right up, he pushed me down against the ladder I'd stood on to reach the meter. I screamed, 'What are you doing? What do you want?' He said, 'I'm after money.' He was trying to put some cotton wool over my mouth which smelled of spirits. I was trying to keep his hand away from my face. I was saying, 'We haven't got any money, we haven't got anything you can steal,' and he said, 'Shut up or I'll kill you.' I then said, 'Let me go into the bathroom and you can search the house and take what you want.' Instead of replying he pushed me into the bathroom and from there into the bedroom. I fell down on the floor. I had the cotton wool in my hands and he was trying to get it.

I kept moving it from hand to hand and then I lost it. He then grabbed both of my hands and tied them behind my back, and put a handkerchief into my mouth, and tied something around my mouth. He picked me up and threw me on the bed. In the struggle my hands became untied but he tied them up again. I had the impression that he was wearing gloves.

When I was lying on the bed he lifted my legs up. I was lying on my back. He pulled my dressing gown open, lifted my legs up over my head and put his hands on my throat. His penis was stiff and he tried to push it into my vagina. At first I thought he was trying to push it up my bottom. But shortly after he came close to the vagina and put it in — a little bit at first. I screamed and said,

29

'You are hurting me.' He didn't say anything. He pushed it further up. Finally he said, 'That's good'. I said nothing, and so he began intercourse. He pressed harder on my throat and I tried to persuade him to take his hands away. I succeeded.

He stopped pushing into my vagina. He stopped pushing his penis in, and he said, 'You're a virgin, aren't you?' I didn't know what he wanted me to say and I didn't want to annoy him, so I said nothing. He then took my left breast and put it in his mouth. I screamed. He continued intercourse but shortly after that he stopped. After a while he moved away and said, 'Get into bed.' I thought he was going to get into bed with me so I sat up. He put all the bedclothes over my head. I thought he was going to suffocate me, but he was just trying to hold me down. I lifted the covers and could see a silhouette of him. I don't think he was wearing any trousers because his legs were so thin. Through a hole in the blankets I could see but I didn't want him to know my hands were now loose. I couldn't see anything clearly but I daren't move. When I couldn't see him anymore, I could hear him moving around the rooms.

Finally I heard him go into the bathroom, and when I couldn't hear him any more I leapt out of bed. I still had my one hand free. I ran down the stairs. I was sure he'd try to catch me. I came down and ran to the front door, but I couldn't open it. Perhaps it was bolted. But I ran to the back door and, when I opened it, I saw him come running down the stairs. I heard him coming after me to the back door, but I had already run out and was standing and hammering on my neighbour's door; and when she opened it I found I had a pair of tights tied round my neck and round my wrists.

I recall that, after he had sex with me, I felt a stabbing pain in my vagina — it hurt. I don't know if he reached orgasm or not inside me. I can only describe him slightly. He was about 5ft 7ins, not a tall man but slimly built and with shoulder-length hair. I think he was in some sort of jacket, and I think he was wearing gloves except when his hands were round my throat. I believe he spoke with a local accent, and I think he was in his early twenties."

So the police now knew they were dealing with a short, local man who was clearly expert at breaking and entering. Indeed it was later learned that the rapist had burgled Anne's house previously, so he knew his way around. Apparently he was now acquiring a taste for rape, and for his next attack he selected Huntingdon Road, a long thoroughfare where numerous houses were occupied by single girls who were often alone at home.

For the female residents of Cambridge, anxieties were starting to grow — especially on the following Friday evening, since the two rapes seemed to be forming a pattern. But there was little they could do except make sure their doors and windows were locked — nobody knew yet that such precautions were of little use in view of the rapist's housebreaking skills.

But the rapist did not strike on the following Friday — instead he waited three more days till Monday 11th November, and then made some bad miscalculations by altering his modus operandi and by attacking a feisty Australian.

Chapter 3
The third attack

On Tuesday November 12th, the *Cambridge Evening News* carried a report of the third attack, in a surprisingly small article: its size was clearly linked to the fact that the police, at least officially, saw no reason to link the incident with the two rapes:

Girl fights attacker

Cambridge police were today hunting a man who fought with a young woman on the doorstep of her home in Huntingdon Road last night. The man, said by police to have been wearing little else but a blanket and wig, ran off after the struggle.

The girl, who was only slightly hurt, answered a knock on her front door at 8.50 p.m. She opened it and found a man standing on the doorstep.
The man spoke briefly and then there was a tussle, said police. The incident follows two recent sexual attacks by a man on young women alone in their homes in Cambridge. But a police spokesman said there was nothing to link it with the other assaults.

The rapist had clearly changed his methods quite radically on this occasion, but there was surely enough in the description given by 29-year-old Elizabeth C, the intended victim, to suggest that the same man as before was involved. She was an Australian touring the world, who had taken a job as a secretary to finance her stopover. According to her account:

"Behind my flat there's a back garden, where there's a footpath down to the garages which abut onto Westfield Lane. One of the garages belongs to my flat, and I always park my car in it. I drive in from Westfield Lane and go out through a door into the back garden. This back door to the garden is always open. As a rule, the garage door out to Westfield Lane is locked, but I'm not certain I locked it that evening.

I got home from work about 6.50 p.m., parked my car in the garage, and went through the back garden into my flat. I called my cats and put them out in the garden. When I'd taken off my coat, I did some ironing in the kitchen. Two hours later I was still ironing when I heard some noise in the garden. I assumed it was my cats making the noise, and went out and called them, but they didn't come. While I was standing out there, I thought I heard a rattling noise, like someone scrambling over the fence into my next door neighbour's garden. I didn't think much of it, I may have been mistaken; and, as my cats weren't in sight, I went in again.

I locked the kitchen door and went on ironing. About twenty minutes later the door bell rang, and when I opened it I saw a man standing there. He was wearing a light brown shoulder length wig, curly in style and very untidy, as if it had been put on very quickly. He had a grey knitted scarf over the lower part of his face, but I couldn't see what else he was wearing because he was holding up a white blanket in front of him. He threw the blanket at me in an attempt to put it over me but it fell at my feet. He said, 'Don't scream. I've got Blackie.' My cat!

He was wearing only a light brown and white jacket and had black PVC or leather gloves, with black knitted pieces down the fingers. Apart from that he was naked. I started to scream and he pushed me very hard into the kitchen, forcing me to crash into the edge of the kitchen sink with such force I thought I had broken it. He grabbed me round the throat and we struggled. I tried to get him out. I was screaming the whole time, and at one point I got him out through the kitchen door into the yard, but he pushed me hard inside again.

He fell against the ironing board and his wig slid a little to the side. The iron fell to the floor. He grabbed the iron — it was still switched on and he must have burned his wig on it judging by the burned nylon I found afterwards. He threatened me with the iron. When he picked it up, I got a chance to get off the floor — he'd thrown me down. I lunged straight at him, screamed and kicked him in the general area of the groin. He grunted so I assumed that I had connected. It looked as if it had paralysed him a bit.

He grabbed the flex of the iron and pulled it out of the socket, and switched off the kitchen light, but I could still see him dimly because a little light was getting in through the door. Suddenly he was fumbling for the door when I pushed him outside and shouted, 'Get out, you bastard.' I don't remember whether his wig came off or I threw it out after him, but I couldn't find it afterwards.

The last I saw of him, he was running through the back garden down to the garage. I ran into my bedroom and hammered on the walls to my neighbours, while screaming for help. A girl called Linda and her fiancé, who were both in the house next door, came to me. I told them what had happened and we rang the police.

Afterwards I could see that the blanket he had with him, and that he left behind, came from a cardboard box in the garage. Then I found a sort of fur-muff which looked as if it belonged to a woman's coat. It was lying on the kitchen floor. I hadn't seen it before, so he must have left it behind.

He was about 30, 5 ft 6 ins. tall and slimly built with short straight black or dark brown hair and maybe unshaven. He was fairly thin, with high cheek bones, a pale, sallow complexion and he spoke in a quiet voice without any noticeable accent. I got the feeling he was a bit effeminate, crossing his hands when he put them on my throat.

I wasn't sexually assaulted and I would do anything to help catch him, but I don't know if I would recognise him again."

Elizabeth was unable to be of more help in the manhunt, as she had already bought her ticket for the journey home to Australia, via America, for two weeks later.

One assumes that the rapist must have used the garage to undress before the attack, and needed to escape by that route in order to retrieve his clothes.

It is hard to believe that the police did not, in fact, immediately link this attack with the two rapes — the man's short stature and slim build, the shoulder-length hair, the grey scarf across the lower mouth, the hands around the throat... Once they decided that the same man was indeed responsible, Elizabeth's account provided them with several vital new clues: her assessment of his age was closer to reality than in the first two accounts, although it was still far short of the mark; she had shown that the long hair was a wig, and so could describe his real hair; and her assessment of his effeminate nature was to prove particularly astute.

On the other hand, the rapist was now aware that the police had a reasonably good description of him — although the photofit picture that was immediately issued, based on Elizabeth's description, looked nothing like him at all. Nevertheless, the fact that she saw him in good light made it necessary to disguise himself more effectively in future. Perhaps due to the frustration and humiliation he had suffered at Elizabeth's hands, he struck again only forty-eight hours later, and this new attack not only involved a far less formidable victim but also showed a marked increase in violence and sadism. It was this fourth attack which marked the true watershed in the case, triggering real panic in the city.

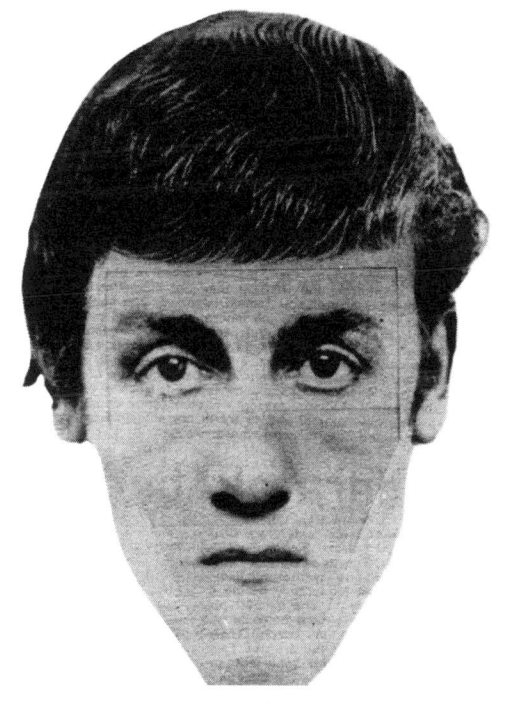

The first police photofit

Chapter 4
The fourth attack

The fourth attack, and the third rape, was a particularly nasty episode which showed that even students in colleges were not safe. So far, girl students had felt reasonably secure, since the first three attacks had taken place in "bedsitland" in the north of the city. But now, for the first time, the rapist hit in the south, and inside a college — Homerton Ladies' College, a teacher-training institution on Hills Road.

The *Cambridge Evening News* of November 14th carried a much bigger headline and article than hitherto, a mark of the increasing severity of the case, as well as of the growing realisation that a serial rapist was at large:

FOURTH CITY SEX ATTACK

An 18-year-old Homerton College student was beaten up and raped last night in the most savage of a recent series of sex attacks on girls in Cambridge. She was raped in a shed in the college grounds. The girl's ordeal began when she was on her own in the sound-proofed music room inside the college.

She was first aware of her attacker's presence when the lights went out, police said today. The man grabbed her and pulled her screaming into the grounds where he beat her. He took her to a remote wooden shed away from the main college buildings where he assaulted and raped her. The man ran off and the girl staggered back to the main buildings where she called for help to two students. They took the girl... to the porter's lodge and he called the police. The attack happened between 8.30 and 9 p.m. It is at about this time that the other attacks have occurred.

The article revealed for the first time that, after the initial attack, the police had set up a special squad working from an incident room at Parkside divisional headquarters. It also acknowledged that the third attack was the rapist's work, only two days after denying it! Due to the viciousness of the fourth attack, the police "are stepping up their inquiries. They have a 100% arrest record in rape cases in Cambridge in recent years."

Another first was that the article was illustrated with two photos of the policemen heading the inquiry — Detective Inspector Jack Cole and Detective Superintendent Bernard Hotson. It was the latter who was destined to become the figurehead of the operation. Aged 49, he had already been on the force for almost thirty years, mostly in East Anglia. The head of Cambridgeshire CID, Detective Chief Superintendent Charles Naan, 47, had joined the Manchester City force twenty-three years earlier, and advanced from detective to DCS (the highest provincial CID rank) in just ten years. He died in 1991. Both men lived just outside Huntingdon, and both had daughters in their twenties. Naan announced that he was strengthening his special squad by bringing in three detective sergeants from the Regional Crime Squad and boosting the manpower to twenty. These officers would be engaged on nothing else but these inquiries. "This man must be found and we will be making a determined effort to this end". The inquiry was being led by Cole, and supervised by Hotson who was deputy commander of Cambridgeshire CID. Rapidly, however, Cole dropped out of the inquiry and instead "minded the shop", directing investigations into the other, more normal crimes happening in Cambridge.

Police briefing with Chief Superintendent Charles Naan and Detective Superintendent Bernard Hotson

Once again, a warning was issued by DCS Naan that "young women should make sure that doors and windows are securely locked and bolted when they are at home or on their own." Needless to say, sales of locks, bolts and door-chains began to rise significantly in the city.

Understandably, the brief report in the newspaper did not reveal the true extent of the terrifying ordeal of this sensitive, slightly-built fresher. According to Janet D's own account:

"I had finished playing the piano about 8.20, got my cello out of the case and began practising with my back to the door in one of the sound-proofed music rooms we call cells. About five minutes later the lights went out. I went to the window, pulled back the curtains and looked out to see if the lights had also gone out in the other rooms, but they hadn't. I went to the door and out into the corridor. There was no light there either. Suddenly someone sprang out of the next cell and pounced on me, put a right arm round my shoulder and a piece of material or rag against my mouth and nose. I was hit by an unpleasant clinical smell. I tried to get free, took a step back, got my mouth free and screamed out, 'Who are you?' I started struggling and he pushed me back into the music cell. I screamed again, 'What do you want?'

He started saying repeatedly, 'I'm going to murder you,' and I was screaming all the time, 'Why? No, please don't. Leave me alone'. He tried again to press the rag, or whatever it was, against my mouth. I screamed again, and he was trying to pin me to the floor, still trying to hold the material over my face. I asked him why he wanted to murder me and he replied, 'I'm not going to murder you but I will if you don't shut up.' He told me to roll over on to my front and he tried to twist my arms behind my back. I resisted, so he said, 'I'll kill you if you don't cooperate. I've come to steal. I'm the raper not a murderer.' I kept asking him questions because I didn't believe him.

He asked me how much my fiddle was worth and when I said it was worth £300 if you take the lot, he said '£300. That's not much, sister.' He twisted me down to the floor, but I said it was the truth, I didn't have any more. He snarled, 'Get up'. He tied my hands behind my back with something made of nylon, and he had to help me up. When I asked him where he was taking me, he said, 'It's all right, I used to work here. I know my way about. I'm taking you where you can't get me into any trouble.' He put something — I thought it was a sack — over my head. He ordered me to take some clothes off, and then he held me tightly at the neck and gagged me, so I could hardly speak. 'If you scream I'll murder you,' he said, 'I've got a big knife'. He was pushing me from behind, out of the cell, along the corridor, out of the building.

I whimpered, 'Where are you taking me?' and, seeing the path led to the Cambridge-London line, I said, 'No, not on the railway lines.' He said 'No, not on the railway lines'. He walked behind me and pushed me forward. I realised we were coming to a grassy area, then down a slope, and into a shed where I bumped into something. He put me down on dry ground, half lying on my back, half on my side, and asked if I had tights on. When I said 'Yes' he said, 'I'm going to tie your legs with them.'

He pushed me down on all fours. I felt his hand pressing on my panties, and then he tore them off. he pulled my jumper up over my head, and then he stayed silent for a while. I asked, 'What are you doing?' and he replied, 'Opening my trousers.' He pushed my shirt and bra up over my breasts. He lay over me, and I felt his hand grope my left breast. I could feel his penis. I was crying, and complained that it was painful to be like that, and it was cold.

He pushed my legs up towards my head and I could feel his penis — which was stiff — push against my body, up behind and between my buttocks. When he pushed himself in, I couldn't help but let out a little scream. I couldn't see anything. The bag was still over my head. But I could feel his breath on my neck. He pushed his penis in and out. It was dreadfully painful. But then he stopped. He pulled out his penis, but only to put it in my vagina.

Shortly afterwards he came. He then changed his manner. He asked what I was called, and I told him 'Janet.' He called me 'baby'. He suggested we went back to his place, a building yard. I asked him, 'Why?' and he said, 'It would be nice and warm, baby.' He got up, got dressed, asked me how much my watch was worth and when I said £50 he would not believe me. But he took it. He said I should remain lying there and wait till he came back; he wanted to take me with him.

He kept telling me to keep still and said, 'I'm going back to get your fiddle and then we'll go back to my place.' I made no attempt to move for about five minutes, half trying to loosen my hands, but frightened in case he returned. I gave him a bit longer, then I counted to 500 and was able to get free and took the sack off. I ran along Pauper's Walk, met two other girls, and they took me to the porter for help, and he telephoned the police."

Due to the darkness, Janet was obviously unable to provide a physical description of her attacker, but her ordeal had some aspects that were fully consistent with the earlier rapes — the emphasis on stealing, the attempted use of some kind of chemical-soaked rag, the threat of a knife (as in the first attack), and above all the act of sodomy which he had attempted unsuccessfully in both the earlier rapes.

There was a definite pattern emerging in his behaviour, although amateur sleuths like myself were as yet totally unable to theorise simply because none of the details of the incidents had been made public. The newspaper articles told us almost nothing. Nonetheless, stories were starting to circulate throughout the city and the university communities, including a rumour that the latest attack had involved a particularly nasty case of sodomy. Naturally, this only served to increase the feelings of acute anxiety among the female population, especially as even colleges could no longer be considered safe havens.

It was in this context of growing anxiety that the *Cambridge Evening News* ran a series of articles by Pauline Hunt two weeks later devoted to the phenomenon of rape and what women should do to protect themselves from it, how they should act in the event of being raped, and how to cope with the ordeal of helping police with investigation and prosecution. She interviewed DCS Naan for his thoughts on these subjects. He made the point that after the initial reporting of an attack, many women go through a very bad patch, and may want to drop the case because they do not want to face the ordeal of testifying in court. Another common reaction to rape is a feeling of being unclean, and the instant reaction may be to bathe — the worst possible thing they can do, from the police's point of view, since the body may retain vital traces which could help identify the man — traces of hair or clothing, his blood group (and today, of course, his DNA).

Chief Superintendent Naan revealed (*CEN* November 28th) that before the attacks by the rapist there had been eleven rapes reported in the Cambridgeshire CID area in 1974, with 100 per cent detection; in 1973 there had been fourteen, again with 100 per cent detection. But he was concerned by the behaviour of some girls in Cambridge who did not seem to realise the seriousness of the current situation — the night after the Homerton rape was reported in the press, girls were still standing under the shadow of trees in Hills Road, thumbing lifts within yards of where the attack took place. He stressed that girls should not put themselves in a situation where they are totally unprotected, and should therefore not accept lifts from strangers, and should exercise caution with men they were "not sure of".

He was asked if women should carry a whistle, or learn some simple karate. His reply was cautious, as this was entering the "have a go" area. A woman's ability to fight off an attacker depends entirely on the particular circumstances — not just her own physical ability, but also the attacker's strength, determination and mental state. "If a woman is so terrified that she may be fatally injured then, of course, rape becomes in these circumstances the lesser of two evils."

"Naturally", he went on "prevention is always far better than fighting for your honour at the last minute." When asked about judo, his reply was that he was not against girls learning some form of self-defence. "I'm neither enthusiastic nor unenthusiastic about judo. It has a value, but I would always advise against putting yourself in the situation in the first place." He pointed out that if somebody struck a woman on the back of the head she would not be able to reach for her whistle or use any judo holds. In short, it was far better to avoid lonely places, and keep home doors and windows locked.

Sound advice, but not, alas, enough to keep the rapist at bay. For his next attack, he returned to house-breaking in bedsitland — and for the first time he used his knife.

Chapter 5
The fifth attack

For his fifth attack, the rapist reverted to his original pattern — a night-time break-in to a flat; but this time it happened on a Saturday, in the Newnham area (the western part of the city, off Barton Road), and in the middle of the night rather than during the evening. Such was the impact of this event that the *Cambridge Evening News* not only put a big headline and story on its front page on December 9th, but it also used — for the very first time — the name by which he would henceforth be known.

CAMBRIDGE RAPIST CLAIMS VICTIM NO. 4

The rapist terrorising girls in Cambridge's bedsit land claimed his fourth victim in two months when he struck in the Newnham area of the city early yesterday... In the latest attack, sometime after 2 a.m., a 21-year-old student was asleep in a bed in a block of flats in Newnham when she was awakened by the rapist. He had got into the flats through the back door. He held a knife to her throat and took her out to the back garden where she was raped.

The article went on to reveal that the special police squad assigned to the case was now twenty-strong; and Detective Superintendent Hotson did not mince his words in describing the man they were seeking: "We are looking for an extremely sick and dangerous man. We believe he is highly intelligent, but with a completely split personality. This man may well commit these vicious attacks, then return home acting completely normally. We are fairly certain he does not drink, so these offences are not the result of over indulgence. He is a man with a vicious streak and a sick mind. We want him badly, but our inquiries are hampered by the fact that he always operates in complete darkness, and without any set pattern."

A few clues were also mentioned for the first time at this point: it was reported that, from the site of the Homerton attack, the police recovered a silk scarf which had yielded some clues after forensic examination. The police were "also making inquiries into one or two other matters connected with the man's possible employment, and they have leads, the nature of which they are not disclosing, on his physical state of health." As always, they appealed for anyone with information to come forward, especially a mother or wife or someone who knew him, and who had noticed him coming home in the early hours of Sunday morning, against his usual habit. In May 1975 it was revealed that a neighbour had heard the rapist and his victim talking in the garden, but thought they were a courting couple and did not want to interfere!

The girl asked the police to shield her identity, so the name of her college was not revealed at the time, and nor was the location in Owlestone Road of the block of flats involved. It later emerged that she was a fourth-year student teacher at Homerton. According to Elizabeth E's own account:

"I came home about 11.30. I let myself in through the front door, closed and locked it after me, and went up to bed in my room, which is the first one you come to when you go upstairs. It was just after midnight when I put on a calf-length night dress with long sleeves and a pair of knickers and went to bed. I lay and read in bed for some time. It must have been 2.30 a.m. when I switched off the light and went to sleep. I don't know how long I had been asleep when suddenly something woke me, I don't know what it was.

My bed stood along one wall, and I could see the window from the bed. The door was in the same wall that my bed stood against, and it opened inwards. I sleep with my feet towards the door.

I opened my eyes. I saw the door open, and I saw a weak light, like the light from a little electric torch, and suddenly I saw a figure who seemed to be holding it. I couldn't see if it was a man or a woman. At first I thought it was one of the other girls who was having problems with the lights in the house. I said, 'Who is it?' and tried to turn on my bedside light but it didn't work. Then I heard a man's voice say, 'Don't scream. I've got a knife, so be quiet.' He was standing between the bed and the door. In an effort to make conversation, I said, 'Who are you?' He replied, 'I'm James.' At the same time he was coming closer. He had switched off the torch, and there was only a bit of light coming in from outside. He put his left hand behind my head, and stretched his right hand forward carefully. He had a cloth or suchlike in his hand, and it smelt a bit like a laboratory. He tried to stuff the cloth into my mouth. He ordered me, 'Open your mouth! Do as I say!' he said harshly, 'Remember, I've got a knife.'

I said, 'I'll do what you want,' and I tried to turn my head away. 'I won't try and scream, I don't need that.' He may have shifted the cloth into his other hand, because now he was touching my cheek with the knife. I stuck my hands up. I touched the knife blade, and it was sharp and curved. I was constantly trying to persuade him to stop stuffing the cloth into my mouth, but he pricked me with the knife, and I realised it was better to let him do as he wanted. I willingly opened my mouth and he popped the cloth in. I couldn't feel anything. I became doped by what I'd first thought I'd smelt.

He asked, 'Have you any money I can steal?' I mumbled, 'No,' and shook my head. 'If I had, I'd give it to you.' He snarled, 'You're lying,' but I repeated what I'd just said. He ordered me onto my stomach, and I obeyed. As I lay down carefully on the cushions, he took the blanket off. I heard him move round the room, and I heard him rummage in my chest of drawers. He opened drawers, but didn't make much noise. Then he came back to the bed. I was still lying on my stomach. I hadn't dared move, and I'd not been able to see what he was doing.

He tied a pair of tights, which he'd obviously taken from my chest of drawers, in front of my eyes. Then he tied my wrists behind my back with another pair of tights. I lay like that while he searched through the rest of the room. I can remember that I tried to spit the cloth out of my mouth, and thought of getting over to the window and screaming for help.

Suddenly he came back and asked if I'd like to go out for a walk. I mumbled a sort of 'No' through the cloth. I can't remember if he forced me up with the knife or if it was only something I imagined. Actually I didn't see any knife at first. But I got off the bed, and I think he pulled me, and then pushed me to the door.

He prodded me with the knife and made me walk downstairs in the dark. We came into the living room, where he said he wanted to lock me in a garden shed, while he searched through the house, but I said there was only a lean-to for bicycles. He took me roughly by the left arm and dragged me out to the back door, while I asked him to stop. I was crying as well. When we came to the back door, I tried to scream. It was hard, as I still had the cloth in my mouth. I tried to spit it out, but he held me in front of my mouth and stuffed it farther in. He shoved me outside and down the path which led down to the little road behind the house.

I was trying to get rid of the gag, but he took more tights from the washing line and lashed them very tightly across my eyes. I couldn't see at all now. I think I trembled, and he asked, 'What's the matter?' I said, 'I'm frightened.' 'Frightened? What of?' 'I don't know what you want to do with me.' 'What do you think?' he asked ironically. 'Are you going to rape me?' I asked, but he didn't answer. He pushed me down to a place — I fell on something that seemed like a bit of grass at the edge of the path. I tried to keep my legs together, but he pulled up my knees so that I was lying on all fours. He didn't say anything. He spread my legs and pulled down my knickers, while he pushed my night dress up to my head. Then he ripped my night dress up the side with his knife, so it hung in bits around my wrists, and he tore my knickers to shreds, and finally I lay totally naked.

Then he suddenly asked, 'Are you cold?' I nodded my head. He ordered me to stand up again, and he put something which I think was a quilt around me — he took it from the washing line. Then he shoved me forward to the path, and talked the whole time about 'knife'. I went down to the path, but I'd lost my sense of direction, so I don't know where we went. I think we came out to the little road.

'I'm scared too,' he said. 'Scared of trouble coming, understand?' Shortly after, he shoved me down again. He rolled me around so I was lying on the quilt. I lay on my back and I heard him rummaging with his clothes. Then he came on top of me. I could feel his stiff penis pushing between my legs. He nipped one of my breasts with his lips. Shortly after, he forced me onto my stomach. I could feel his penis up between my legs, which I was trying to keep together. He again turned me onto my back, and forced my legs apart, and shoved them up, so my knees were up by my shoulders.

He held me tight like that, and I could again feel his penis pushing. Suddenly it slid up into my vagina. He made the movements of intercourse, and I don't know how long it lasted. I didn't detect whether he came, but when he later pulled himself out and I got up to a standing position, I felt something run down to my thigh.

When he began to push his penis up, I mumbled to him that I had a Tampax in there. 'You're lying,' he said. Perhaps he tried to feel for it, but he just carried on and forced himself right up me. I don't think he took very long. Afterwards he asked if I'd enjoyed it. I heard him adjusting his clothes. Then he suggested we should stroll down to the river Cam. I shook my head. At one moment he'd told me 'I've got VD.' When I said, 'Oh have you?' and told him I was ill, he said, 'You're a liar.'

He asked, 'Are you going to the police?' When I lied and said, 'No,' he said 'Of course you are', and I said, 'Yes!' He pressed the knife into my skin, I think, and I again said 'No, no, I won't go to the police.' 'If you do, I'll come back at night, so you'd best let things drop.' He described in unflattering terms the full police physical examination and said, 'If you go to the police they will look in your knickers and look up inside you.'

He shoved me again, and we set off. I think we returned to the garden behind the house. He stood still, and I thought he was going to kill me. 'I've got a car out in the street, and I'll be in London before you can fetch help from anywhere.'

I found myself in the garden. I heard no footsteps, and I didn't hear a car start, but I did hear a rattle like the noise of a bicycle chain. I got into the house, finding my way by touch, and freed my hands with great difficulty. I ran up to my friend Diana, but she wasn't home. Just then, the two other girls came who also have rooms in the house. We tried to phone the police, but our phone was out of action, so we had to go the phone box.

He had a slight Fenland accent, but he sounded as if he were trying to play the stage villain in a play."

Once again, due to his cutting the electricity and causing total darkness, there was no physical description available from this episode, but nevertheless some important points emerged. First, the confirmation that he had a reasonably local accent. And above all, the clue that he was using a bicycle. None of the other victims had mentioned hearing a car driving away, and the very fact that he went out of his way to tell this girl that he had a car made it pretty obvious that he did not — why mention it, if not to try to lay a false trail? The name "James" was undoubtedly another lie — why would he give his real name? One puzzling aspect was the continuing attempt to use a spirit-soaked rag — as this had had no effect on any of the earlier victims, why did he persist with it?

It is also intriguing to reflect that he had probably read with keen interest the articles on rape by Pauline Hunt which had appeared in the local newspaper just over a week before. One of the points she had emphasised is how the awful prospect of the new ordeal of undergoing a physical examination often makes victims think twice about reporting the offence, and presumably this is why he mentioned it to the girl. Perhaps he was hoping this would be enough to deter her from going to the police.

However, the most alarming aspect of the fifth attack was undoubtedly the fact that the knife, only mentioned as a threat in the past, had now come into play. Perhaps it was simply his way of forcing the girl to succumb to having the cloth in her mouth. Be that as it may, it was henceforth to be a standard feature of his attacks.

The very next day after reporting the fifth attack, the *Cambridge Evening News* carried an article — entitled "Boyfriends can help stop the rapist — police chief" — which, in a way, was quite historic. As far as I am aware, this was the very first time that the British police actively recommended that single girls should encourage their boyfriends to spend the night. The advice was given by Detective Superintendent Hotson. It was unquestionably a very sensible course of action, and done with the best possible intentions, but at the time it caused something of a scandal among, on the one hand, those with religious or moral objections and, on the other, the more extreme feminists in the city who felt insulted that women's safety should be thought to be dependent on the male sex. I well remember the lively discussions in student common rooms about Hotson's recommendation. However, he has informed me that he never received any protests about the matter.

What he advised was this: a male presence could be seen as a deterrent to attacks by the rapist, so single girls living alone in the city might consider asking their boyfriends to spend the night in their flat, or work out alarm codes to alert their neighbours. "One of the best deterrents is having a man about the house. It is our experience that the vast majority of young people living away from home in bedsitters or flats are responsible in the way they conduct their lives... I do not wish to become involved in questions of morality, but the evidence is that the presence of a male in the immediate vicinity is a very good deterrent against this type of attacker. I believe that young people living away from home these days are quite capable of making their own decisions on these questions. My only interest is in protecting these girls from a particularly nasty form of attack."

The rapist's method of operating so far had shown that he had never attacked where he knew there was a man in the house or the immediate vicinity, and it was for that reason alone that Hotson made his recommendation. He pointed out that there were many houses in Cambridge where men and women were living in the same building, and at times like these one could say that mixed tenancy was a blessing. Where large houses were split into flats, he suggested that codes should be worked out between girls living alone and men in other parts of the house. "If they could work out some system of communication which would alert the man to the girl's predicament without rousing the suspicion of the attacker, this could prove to be a very worthwhile preventive measure."

Boyfriends can help stop the rapist—police chief

A police chief hunting the Cambridge rapist hinted last night that single girls living alone in the city might consider asking their boyfriends to spend the night in their flats, or work out alarm codes to alert their neighbours.

The idea was hinted at by Det. Supt. Bernard Hotson, who heads the special 20-man squad set up to hunt the rapist, and came after the attacker claimed his fourth victim in the early hours of Sunday morning in a bedsitter in Newnham.

Last night in suggesting ways single girls could protect themselves, Det. Supt. Hotson said: "One of the best deterrents is having a man about the house. It is our experience that the vast maj-

Male presence seen as deterrent to city attacks

ority of young people living away from home in bedsitters or flats are responsible in the way they conduct their lives.

Asked if he was suggesting that single girls should ask their boyfriends to spend the night in their flats, Det. Supt. Hotson said: "I will say this, I do not wish to become involved in questions of morality, but the evidence is that the presence of a male in the immediate vicinity is a very good deterrent against this type of attacker.

"I believe that young people living away from home these days are quite capable of making their own decisions on these questions. My only

interest is in protecting these girls from a particularly nasty form of attack."

The rapist's method of operating has shown that he has never attacked when he has known a man was in the house or in the immediate vicinity.

"It is for this reason and for this reason alone that I say a man about the house at this particular time is one of the best deterrents." Mr. Hotson said.

He pointed out that there were many houses in Cambridge where men and women were living in the same building, and added: "It is at times like these when one could say a mixed tenancy is a blessing."

Living alone

Where large houses were split into flats, he suggested that codes should be worked out between girls living alone and men in other parts of the house.

"If they could work out some system of communication which would alert the man to the girl's predicament without rousing the suspicion of the attacker, this could prove to be a very worthwhile preventive measure."

Because the rapist always operates under cover of complete darkness, even making sure the light switches are well out of the reach of his victim, he suggested that girls should keep a heavy torch by their beds both to see the attacker with and use as a weapon in self defence.

"It is important also that should any girl return to her flat and find that either the lighting or the telephone has been interfered with, they should contact us immediately," he said.

If they returned late at night and the lights were

Supt. Hotson

not working, they should leave the flat immediately without investigating the cause in case the attacker was already inside.

The rapist, who police described yesterday as "intelligent but vicious and sick," has attacked five girls raping four of them in the last two months. His favourite method is to overpower the girl indoors and then rape her outside.

Police believe he takes great care in selecting his victims possibly spending quite some time observing both the area and then the actual block of flats or bedsitters where his victim lives.

"There are many flats in the city where the occupants clearly indicate on the nameplates that they are female and single. In these cases we advise girls to change the style on their nameplates giving only their surname.

"Positive effort should be made to see that all doors and windows are securely locked, and that all external gates and doors into and out of yards or gardens are locked. Any cycles left lying outside should either be locked or taken in doors. It is important that his man's life should be made as difficult as possible either in getting into flats or getting away after he has attacked," Mr. Hotson said.

Because the rapist always operated under cover of complete darkness, even making sure the light switches were well out of reach of his victims, Hotson sensibly suggested that girls should keep a heavy torch by their beds both to see the attacker with, and perhaps dazzle him, and to use as a weapon in self-defence. "It is important also that should any girl return to her flat and find that either the lighting or the telephone has been interfered with, they should contact us immediately. If they returned late at night and the lights were not working, they should leave the flat immediately without investigating the cause in case the attacker was already inside." All of this was very sound advice, in that era long before mobile phones.

Finally, Hotson pointed out that the rapist seemed to take great care in selecting his victims, possibly spending quite some time observing both the area and then the actual block of flats or bedsitters where his victim lived. "There are many flats in the city where the occupants clearly indicate on the nameplates that they are female and single. In these cases we advise girls to change the style on their nameplates, giving only their surname. Positive effort should be made to see that all doors and windows are securely locked, and that all external gates and doors into and out of yards or gardens are locked. Any cycles left lying outside should either be locked or taken indoors. It is important that this man's life should be made as difficult as possible either in getting into flats or getting away after he has attacked."

Certainly the latter part of Hotson's advice was being taken increasingly seriously in the city, and sales of locks and door-chains continued to soar. Some girls also resorted to simple devices such as putting empty bottles in front of windows, so that anyone coming in by that route would make a loud noise. Others kept open pepper pots by their beds, as pepper in the eyes would put an attacker out of action for a few minutes. And of course, some girls were only too happy to adopt the solution of inviting their boyfriends to stay over, and one imagines that this feeling was reciprocated!

Forty-eight hours later, on December 12th, the newspaper reported that a woman had been attacked at teatime only yards from where the rapist had claimed his fourth victim a few days earlier. She said that the man had put his hand up her clothes. A 30-year-old medical student who was out running on Coe Fen heard her cries and chased the man for a long distance, until he entered a house off Mill Road and escaped through a back door and disappeared in a maze of back gardens. This, however, was a red herring — not only was this completely different behaviour from that of the rapist, but the student described the man as being about 6 ft 3 ins. tall, and wearing a light-coloured raincoat.

Only four days were to pass, however, before the rapist himself struck again, for the last time that year, and closing this first series of attacks. And not only that, he returned to the very same house where the Australian girl had beaten him off. Presumably he did not know she had returned to Australia — this news had not been made public — so perhaps he was seeking to complete unfinished business or have his revenge. Whatever the motive, this attack was to be the worst and most violent yet.

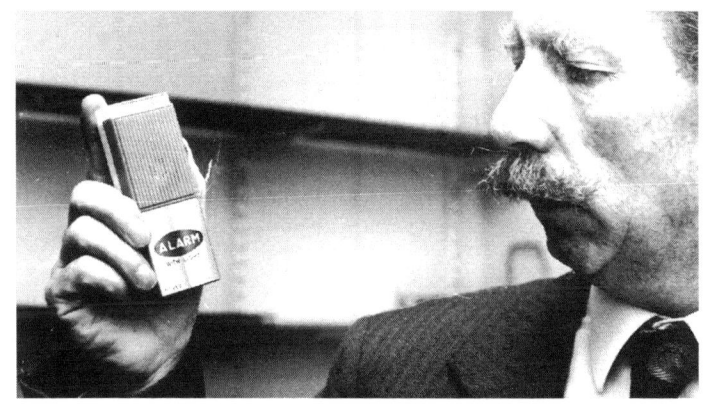

DS Hotson with alarm

Chapter 6
The sixth attack

Once again, the rapist struck in the early hours of a Sunday morning, as in the fifth attack, thus apparently starting a new pattern. On Monday December 16th the *Cambridge Evening News* carried a startling and alarming headline:

RAPIST STABS CITY GIRL IN SIXTH ATTACK

In a savage knife attack, the man terrorising single girls in Cambridge claimed his fifth rape victim early yesterday morning. And it was his second visit to the same house where less than five weeks earlier a girl successfully fought him off on the doorstep. But this time the rapist, wearing a false beard and wig, brutally knifed his 20-year-old victim on the face, hands and arms before raping her in the tiny bedroom of her ground-floor flat in Huntingdon Road.

Not only was this his second visit to that house, but only half an hour earlier he had been frightened off by a man when he broke into 174 Victoria Road. It was later reported that the man woke up and said, "Who's there?", and the rapist replied, "Sorry, wrong house" and went away. The man was staying with his girlfriend, who had thus heeded the police advice to girls in the city to ask their boyfriends to stay the night. It was perhaps because he had been thwarted in this new attempt that the rapist determined to go and seek revenge at the house where he had been fought off before.

Be that as it may, the Scots-born girl, a telephonist, put up a tremendous fight in her flat at 6 Huntingdon Road, just opposite Fitzwilliam College — it was in a shambles, with bloodstained bedclothes and personal effects strewn across the blue mattress which was hanging half off the bed. She had been taken to Addenbrooke's Hospital to have her wounds stitched, and was now staying with friends at a secret address in the city. Her wounds eventually required weeks of hospital treatment.

The attack had happened between 3.30 and 4.45 a.m. After knifing and raping the girl, the rapist, who had got in by forcing a window, escaped by unbolting the door to the flat and running through the garden, as he had done before, to Westfield Lane, which runs at the back of Huntingdon Road. The garden gate had been forced almost off its hinges.

He had left the girl bound, gagged and bleeding. Her flat was at the back of the house, with a separate door. She freed herself, and staggered to the front of the house where she banged on a ground-floor window. According to the woman who lived there, "I opened my door and she collapsed on the floor, covered in blood. I knew what had happened. I had a premonition about it and I had warned the girls here that he would be back. I don't know why, I just knew he would come back." She raised the alarm, and police arrived within minutes. They had been around the corner in Victoria Road, investigating his attempt from earlier that night. But the time it had taken the girl to free herself had given her attacker a head start on the police, and he got clean away.

According to Shelley F's own account:

"I had put on a long night dress and dressing gown and went to bed. I had the radio on to hear the time, and I lay and read a book for about ten minutes before I switched off the light, turned off the electric heater and went back to bed to sleep. A short time later I was woken by hearing some sort of noise — I thought I heard a slight movement in my room, but it may have been the kitten. So I didn't think anything of it, and turned onto my side to go to sleep again. Sometime later I woke up again, and this time I saw the light of an electric torch shining right in my face from a distance of about eighteen inches. There was someone in my room. I suddenly understood that, and I realised it wasn't a girl when he said something to me — something about if I screamed or resisted he would chop my head off. I felt a knife at my throat. I began lifting my head from the pillow, and felt the point. The figure above me moved the knife back as I lifted myself up.

I became wide awake and scared. I thought, 'Oh my God.' I remembered the girl who had the flat before, and all the stuff in the papers. I knew what was going to happen. I grew panic-stricken, and at the same time he had hold of my hair with one hand and was pressing a knife to the back of my neck with the other. The torch was lying and shining somewhere or other. I screamed once, that's all. I didn't think it would do much good doing it again. I wish I had, because someone heard it and thought it was me talking to someone.

I struggled against him. Without thinking of anything else — I just struggled and, as a result, I fell off the bed. I kept on struggling, and didn't think at all about the knife which he was still holding in his hand. While we were struggling like this, we got near to the bedroom door and over the threshold into the kitchen. I was able to switch on the electric light but he was startled and immediately switched it off again.

Nevertheless I managed to get a glimpse of him. I couldn't believe what I was seeing — it was just not human. He was about my height, 5 ft 4 ins. His face, apart from the area around his eyes, appeared to be covered by long hair. It was black and had the texture of straw. It looked rougher than ordinary hair. This mass of hair was dark like a wig, and a beard covered most of his face. When the light went on, I also saw blood on the pillow and the top of the bed. I thought then it was no use and I gave up fighting.

Finally he crushed me up against the door and twisted one of my arms behind my back. Shortly after he also twisted my other arm. He tied my hands behind my back with a pair of my flatmate's undies and a pair of tights which he'd obviously found in the room or had brought with him in his pocket. Breathless, I asked him, 'What do you want? Why are you doing this?' and he said, 'I don't know.' He tried to pull me out of the bedroom and then pushed me back towards the bed. I said I'd stop resisting if he stopped hurting me. I kept asking him how he got in. He didn't say anything for a long time, and then he said, 'I can break in anywhere.' His voice was low and husky. I told him I was not going to struggle.

He shoved me down onto the bed where I ended up half-lying on my back. I told him I couldn't breathe through my nose so he tied a handkerchief in my mouth and round my head. He sat on the bed and, shortly after, stuck his knife in under my night dress and slit it from the hem to the neck. The electric torch was still lying and shining on part of the bed, and it was the only light in the room.

While he was cutting my night dress, he was half-lying over me, and he pulled it apart and exposed the front of my body. When he saw my naked body he leaned back a little. Then he got up. He reached down into some bag and I could hear tools or a bottle rattling before he knelt on the bed and put some cream or vaseline on his fingers and smeared it between my labia. I lay stretched out on the bed. It felt cold, what he smeared on me. Then he lay over me. I think he unfastened his trousers while he lay on one arm. Then I felt his penis against my mons veneris. He lifted up my legs with one hand on each ankle. Then he lay out straight, and then I felt his penis start to push into my vagina.

While he was raping me, he bit me on the breast. I don't think he came. And during all that time he lay on me and made the movements of intercourse and didn't say a word. When he had got out of me, I could raise myself a little, and I saw he was zipping up his trousers. I asked if he would lay a blanket on me, as I was cold. He did so, and it made me think that, although he had cut me in the fight, maybe he hadn't really meant to.

Then he leaned over me and shone the electric torch into my face. He asked if I could untie myself. I said I didn't think I could. He didn't believe me. He said, 'Yes, you can.' Then he said, 'You called me a bastard. You said if you had the knife you would stab me. Well, I have the knife and you got cut.'

I hadn't said anything of the kind. I think he must have got me mixed up with another girl — maybe the girl who had the flat before. Then he said he would go for a moment, but would come back in five minutes. He left, and I thought that he had just gone to the toilet and was coming back — you think these crazy things, I suppose — but shortly after I heard the outer door close, so I now knew he'd left the house.

I lay still and listened for I don't know how long. I knew I could get my right hand free, but my left was firmly tied. I had been cut there as well. When I heard no more sounds, I got up and managed to get my hands loose. I suppose I should have raised the alarm, but I was very shaky and had lost a lot of blood. I just sat on the bed and had a cigarette.

I got off the bed, and tried to switch on the light but it didn't work. I ran out of my bedroom, and tried the light there — it didn't work either, so I turned on the gas cooker to make a bit of light. Then I put on a housecoat and ran over to my neighbour, Mrs Bell, in the dark. I felt awful about waking her up, but I didn't want to stop a car or anything. 'He's been to Huntingdon Road again!' I shouted. 'Who?' Mrs Bell was bewildered, but shortly afterwards she understood. She got up and freed my hands, and she said, 'Him?' 'Yes,' I replied, 'him! I don't know if he had gloves on or not.' I mumbled, and didn't understand myself why I thought of that.

When they switched on the light I could see the cuts and the blood, and I felt sick and thought I would faint. Cuts on my arm and fingers needed many stitches. There was bruising on my neck, back and right leg, and a cut on my cheek just below the right eye. I really thought he was going to kill me."

Almost ten months later, after the rapist's trial, she told journalists: "I will never be normal again. I am a changed person." She had moved to Cambridge from Perth in October 1973 with a friend called Lorna. "We were two teenagers seeking the gay life of independence. That is a faded dream. Now I want security. I want to marry and settle down, but I am not trying to run away from what has happened to me. I am marrying my boyfriend only because I love him. We want to get married as soon as possible." She met her 24-year-old boyfriend, who owned his own business and lived in a village outside Cambridge, on Christmas Eve, nine days after the rape, though they had known each other briefly before. He told the press, "She has changed so much. She gets so depressed. The actual rape itself does not affect her. She would not talk to me at first about what happened."

Shelley explained that she and Lorna moved into the £9-a-week flat only a few days after Elizabeth, the Australian girl, was attacked there in November. "Liz is only 5 ft 2 ins. and very slight, but she fought him off even though, as she told me, she was frightened to death. Now she is in America on her world tour and I have got one of her cat's kittens called MacTavish. When we moved in we made sure there was a chain on the door and an extra lock, and that the windows were secure. We got a telephone and an extension installed.

On the day I was raped, I came home from work at about 4.15 p.m. and went to the shops for the weekend shopping, boiled ham and beans. Lorna was away for the weekend, but I was not worried. You think it happens to everybody else but you. I was reading *Heidi*, of all things, and listening to Neil Diamond on a cassette when I dropped off to sleep. When I woke up it was about 11 p.m. I decided to do some hoovering." After that she went to bed, and the rape took place, as described in her police statement. Afterwards she needed twenty stitches in her arm, eight in her wedding ring finger and five in the index finger of her right hand. "I was out of hospital in a few hours, and went to stay with family friends in Cambridge. The doctor gave me sedatives but I never took them.

My father and mother came down from Scotland and my elder sister from Yarmouth, and they were all amazed at how calmly I was taking things. I was proud of myself. The only thing that upset me was going back to the flat and seeing the mouthpiece off the telephone. I just kicked it into the wall. Everything was still covered in blood. After a while things got worse and I thought I was going to end up in a mental hospital. I would not sleep at nights but stayed awake until dawn. When the doctor sent me to a psychiatrist I thought I had gone mad. But the psychiatrist told me there was nothing he could do for me, and I felt a bit better. I have never shown anybody how frightened I have been. The rape meant nothing to me, that was nothing.

"My boyfriend knows how frightened I have been. When I moved into a house with friends a short while ago I went out and bought a lock for my bedroom door and on the first night I put a dressing table up against the door. If there is a window open I have to shut it. Last night I left the back door open for a while and checked out the whole house before I dared to go to bed. There is no point in leaving Cambridge. I would only be running away. I would not mind settling here with my boyfriend.

It was weeks, maybe months, before I cried. Then I was very upset. It is only these past few weeks that I have been coming round. I still have problems sleeping. I wake up and think it's all happening again. I have my boyfriend now, and everything's fine between us. There are no problems. It is just when you are alone at night. In bed, you know. When you dream it's just like it all over again. You suddenly wake up with the exact same feeling you had when it happened. It's bloody awful."

****

DCS Naan came from his home near Huntingdon to take personal charge — DS Hotson had already been up all night with the 20-man special squad — and announced that he was calling men off other duties to strengthen the manpower of the squad. By the weekend he hoped to have no less than fifty men devoting themselves to nothing else other than catching the man he described as "a monster who is carefully planning his moves. Our job is made doubly difficult because he follows no set pattern. There is nothing to link these attacks either in area, time or type of victim."

The following day the Cambridgeshire Chief Constable, F. Drayton Porter, told the county's Police Committee that "We are certainly looking for a madman. This is one of the most dangerous and the most serious offences I have known in my forty-two years in the force." The man was being hunted with the same single-minded resolve as the force would seek a murderer. Only a few days later it was reported that more than sixty officers, and eventually seventy, were working up to 14 hours a day on the case. Since the manhunt began, police had interviewed over 1000 men and carried out spot checks and street stop-and-search operations on hundreds more. Most people realised that the searches and questionings were necessary and cooperated very well. In addition, the police enlisted the help of psychiatrists and doctors in an effort to get inside the rapist's mind. Their initial assessments were that he was:

- A loner, perhaps living alone or with his mother.
- A non-drinker who has difficulty socializing.
- Uncomfortable in women's company.
- Afraid of women and his apprehension shows.
- The chap who eats alone in works canteen or café.
- He may visit the same cinema every night when a sex film is on the bill.
- If his job is among people, he will always be the one apart from the crowd.
- Alas, the psychiatrists were completely mistaken on all these points.

One interesting footnote at this point is that the police were asked whether they felt that Stanley Kubrick's film *A Clockwork Orange*, of 1971, might have influenced the rapist's behaviour. The film had caused a tremendous furore when it first appeared, and, as is well known, Kubrick himself withdrew it from circulation in Britain after only a year because some copycat attacks had begun to take place. Where the Cambridge rapist was concerned, DCS Naan seems to have felt that there was probably a link. He said that the attacks were "like something from the film 'Clockwork Orange,' where there are scenes of grotesquely made-up men attacking and raping women. We don't know who this man is, so who is to say what has influenced him? What he has been doing around Cambridge is 'Clockwork Orange' all over again. He started off with threats, then a beating, and now he has used a knife."

One major development was that Shelley had managed to get to a light switch and had a good look at him. "The sight that met her must have been grotesque to say the least," said the police. Her assailant was wearing a wig and false beard, as well as a green pullover — which might now be bloodstained — and dark-coloured trousers. The police issued a new photofit picture, which was published in the newspaper article — it showed the man in wig and false beard, and also what he might look like without the beard. The new picture brought in more than 100 calls to the police. However, according to DS Hotson, while people were ringing up with the best of intentions and all information was being followed up, "the response is mostly coming from middle-aged mature residents. We are disappointed that more younger people are not coming forward because it may well be that someone in this age group has got information we want."

Unfortunately, events were to prove that this new photofit, like the previous one, did not bear the slightest resemblance to the rapist. After only one day the police announced that the first photofit was a better likeness because Elizabeth had seen him unbearded in good light. They appealed to the public to keep the image firmly in mind, and indeed to "cut it out and carry it with you. If you see anyone you think answers the description, tell the police immediately."

Shelley confirmed that the rapist was short, about 5 ft 4 ins. tall, and she said that his voice was slightly high-pitched, with a local accent. Unfortunately, she too got his age hopelessly wrong

— she thought he was about twenty-five. This mistake, inevitably, continued to make life miserable for all short young men in Cambridge — everyone used to stare at them in the street, wondering... and of course many of them were questioned repeatedly by police.

Indeed, stories abounded in the student community of police taking advantage of the situation to search numerous rooms, ostensibly in the search for the rapist, but at the same time seeking and finding drugs. I was to experience this myself very soon afterwards during my own interrogation.

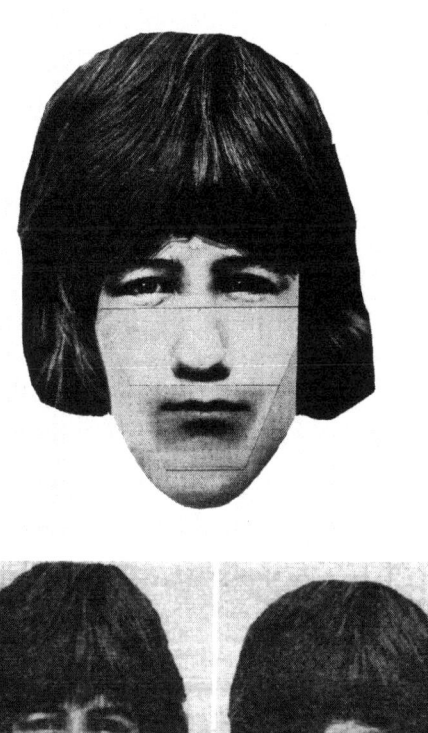

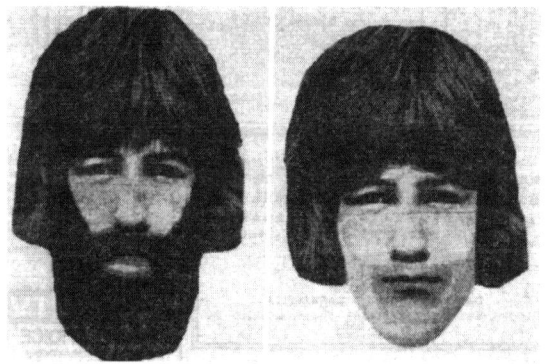

The second police photofit

Chapter 7
The interval

At this point, the saga becomes personal for an instant. As a keen amateur sleuth with a particular interest in serial crimes, I had naturally been following the unfolding events as closely as I could. Inevitably, my only sources of real information were the sparse accounts in the local newspaper, so that, up to and including the report on the fifth attack, I had only been able to deduce that the perpetrator was a short, slim, youngish man, almost certainly local, who rode a bicycle, and who had a detailed knowledge of bedsitland and some expertise not only in housebreaking but also in cutting power- and telephone-lines. Probably not a student, therefore.

Another source of information, albeit far less reliable, was the rumour mill which had been spreading Chinese whispers around the city of Cambridge and through the student community from the time of the second attack onwards. One heard endless stories and theories, and nuggets of news which came from someone who knew someone who knew someone in the police. As we shall see, this phenomenon was to be exacerbated as time went on.

I had returned home to Hull for the Christmas holidays on December 14th, shortly after the fifth attack, and heard about the sixth from the TV news and national press. In early January 1975 I came back to Cambridge, and was anxious to see the full report, such as it was, of the last attack in the *Cambridge Evening News*. At that time the newspaper had a small establishment just off Market Square, where one could examine and buy recent issues, and so I went in there on January 6th to acquire the ones which interested me. In all innocence, I wrote the relevant dates down on the back of an envelope addressed to me in Hull. Such was the state of heightened alertness and anxiety in the population that the lady who took my order thought it suspicious that I wanted these particular issues, and passed my details to the police.

The Cambridge police immediately contacted the Hull police. A detective and a policewoman swiftly called on my parents and asked for my Cambridge address. They assured them it was nothing to worry about, and said that all Cambridge students were being contacted for statements — but they did ask if I had talked about the case while I was at home. Fortunately, their visit did not alarm my parents, because they were well aware, from what I had told them and from what they had seen and heard in the media, that virtually every young male in Cambridge was being checked out in some way. Besides, they knew perfectly well that I was in Hull at the time of the latest attack!

Nevertheless, a few days later on January 9th, at 11.15 a.m., the bell rang in my bedsit in a house owned by Gonville and Caius College in Harvey Road. When I opened the front door I was confronted by two men: "Mr Bahn? CID." As soon as I opened the door, they knew I was not the rapist, simply because I am 6ft 2ins tall, but nevertheless they proceeded to give me a thorough grilling, and to search my room from top to bottom. It took no more than half an hour but felt far longer.

It was not a pleasant experience — acute embarrassment was compounded by an inexplicable sense of unease and guilt, even though I knew I was completely innocent. At the same time, it was fascinating to see the classic "Nice and Nasty" or "Good cop Bad cop" routine being put into action, as one of them went out of his way to be pleasant to me, while the other was extremely curt and aggressive.

As already mentioned, the police were taking advantage of the situation to search for drugs, and that is presumably what they were after in my case — they lifted up my mattress, went through every cupboard and drawer, and even felt up inside an African tom-tom by the fireplace. The main problem, as far as I was concerned, was the range of stuff in my room which could have landed me in very serious trouble had I been shorter.

For a start, I had several sharp knives lying around, as well as a machete from an archaeological expedition to South America. As a student of archaeology, specialising in how prehistoric people exploited animals for food and other materials, I had begun to make a collection of animal bones as an aid to identifying bones and bone-fragments found in archaeological sites. For weeks I had been obtaining fresh bones from the abattoir, from a gamekeeper and from a butcher. I had even shared the cost with a fellow student of acquiring an entire, very bloody, defleshed horse carcass. All these bones had to have the remaining flesh scraped off, and then they had to be boiled and treated with a chemical to emerge nice and clean and white. Some of the boiling had been done on the stove in my bedsit, much to the cleaning lady's horror, when she encountered the smell and the sight one day. Fortunately, I had not yet resumed these activities in early January, but the bones and the sharp knives were in the room on open display.

Second, I had a spare blanket in a holdall on top of my wardrobe, and this looked suspicious since the rapist had worn a blanket during the third attack.

Third, my bookshelf in the bedsit contained not only a study of the Moors Murders, but also a book called *The Social History of*

Rape (by Paul Tabori, 1971), which I had picked up cheap at a sale in mid-November. That too looked incriminating.

Most embarrassing of all, at the back of a drawer was something I had long forgotten — a pair of girl's paper knickers. I have a sister who has lived in Germany since 1969; and after a long spell of not hearing anything from her, I had sent a postcard jokily inscribed "Any chance of some Briefs?" (i.e. letters). She had promptly mailed me these paper knickers in response. I enjoyed the joke, put them away in the drawer, and forgot about them until the detective quietly unfolded them, held them up, raised an eyebrow, and then neatly folded them up and put them back. I tried to explain, but it sounded like a ridiculous story, even to me!

Afterwards, it struck me that, had I been short, there were other factors which might have caused suspicion. For much of that autumn term I had been helping a group of fellow-students with a piece of experimental archaeology — we had constructed a prehistoric kiln, using only original materials (such as an animal dung coating!), on a piece of open ground on the edge of the city, and we had fired some crude pots in it. All that work meant that I had kept some very strange hours, often returning to Harvey Road very late at night or in the early morning. That too would have needed some explaining.

I was quite shaken, but also oddly exhilarated, by the experience of being interrogated, and lost no time in telling my friends and colleagues about it. Needless to say, everyone found it hilarious, and I received no sympathy at all! One friend suggested to me that I was indeed the rapist, but always walked on my knees to disguise my height! I dined out on the incident for a long time.

The archaeology department at that time employed a technician whose son was in the police force, and who was therefore able to give us occasional pieces of information about the case which were obviously more reliable than the usual rumour mill. I therefore asked him if his son could please check how my interrogation had been logged at the station. Apparently I had been described simply as a harmless eccentric with a machete in his room! So that was a relief, albeit slightly upsetting...

After the ferocity of the sixth attack in December, it is very understandable that the atmosphere among female students returning for the January term was one of enormous anxiety. I was seeing a maths student from Newnham College at the time, and she certainly was very apprehensive about returning to Cambridge before the rapist was caught. However we felt sure that she was comparatively safe since she had a room inside the college itself — this was just as well, as I would not have been allowed to spend the night inside the college, despite the police recommendation. Cambridge colleges had not yet become liberal enough for that to be openly accepted.

Everyone waited tensely for the next attack — in which part of the city would he strike? Would it be a student or a "civilian"? Would the violence escalate even further? This last point was obviously the most worrying. Every female student of my acquaintance was extremely anxious, and one actually left Cambridge in a state of some mental distress. The student newspaper *Stop Press* issued a prominent warning under the photofit picture. It declared that the rapist was still at large, though had gone to ground. "It is clear that the attacks are very carefully prepared. The rapist first makes sure that his victims are living alone, and always chooses isolated spots. If there is any danger of his being disturbed he takes the victim out of the house. He takes great care not to be seen, and usually breaks in while the girl is out, sabotages the lights and lies in wait, or he enters while she is asleep. He often wears a false beard or wig, making identification even more difficult. His precautions have been so effective that he has only been seen by two of his victims. A description has, however, been issued, and several forensic clues have been found, but the police are unwilling to discuss these."

The newspaper provided interesting details of how the university was adapting to the situation: "The women's colleges have tightened security on police advice. While individual colleges have different systems, men are allowed in through main entrances only, having to sign in and out, produce identification and give the name of the person they are visiting. If they are not accompanied by a student of the college they may not be let in. The precautions are working well: one woman at Girton came home to find that a man she did not know had signed in to see her. It took him a very long time to convince the police that a friend of hers had asked him to deliver a message."

It was reported that student reactions varied: "At Girton, where the atmosphere is 'edgy' and some women are armed with hat pins and pepper, people are 'very appreciative,' while one comment at Newnham was, 'It's an absolute bind, but necessary if only to put people's minds at rest.'" DS Hotson was quoted as saying that the student attitude was "very responsible. Provided you realise the danger, the thing to do is keep calm and take precautions. While this man is at large, no girl is safe."

But January passed, and then February, and nothing happened. By March, girls in Cambridge were already letting their guard down with a sense of great relief, and the rumour mill really came into its own at this point. I well remember hearing assurances from a wide range of friends and colleagues that the rapist had fled the area, or had committed suicide, or had died, or had been caught and put in a lunatic asylum. In response, I pointed out that the police would certainly have informed the public if any of those scenarios was true, so as to put an end to the terror. However, I knew, thanks to regular reports from my friend, the policeman's father, that the police were still on full alert. They knew that the rapist was still around and could strike at any time. So I did my best to counter the wishful thinking and to spread the word that the threat was still all too real; my girlfriend also passed this on to her friends at Newnham and on her course.

In early January a friend told me that the police knew that the rapist was a man who had been let out of Broadmoor; they surrounded his house, but he escaped through a back window. This had all been hushed up! The story was nonsense, as Bernard Hotson has recently confirmed to me, but some elements of it eventually proved to contain a grain of truth.

Another story that came from my friend, the policeman's father, was that police suspected the rapist might be a student at Fitzwilliam College — this was particularly worrying news for a female friend of mine, whose boyfriend attended that college and did bear some resemblance to the first photofit picture which had been issued! I well remember her crying because she had confided in her tutor, who contacted the police. They promised to be kind to him, accused him of being the rapist, promised him a place in a nice mental home, and took samples of his blood, saliva and hair for tests. He had come to her in tears, but since then had begun to avoid her, presumably because she had confessed that she had reported him. A couple of days later, of course, we learned that his tests had proved negative.

When March too passed without incident one can understand the enormous temptation to assume that the rapist was history, and the sheer relief of choosing to believe that life had returned to normal.

The awful truth was suddenly revealed on April 13th, when another girl underwent a terrifying ordeal. The rapist was back in action, and this time he had altered his appearance yet again.

Chapter 8
The seventh attack

The shock came with a headline in the *Cambridge Evening News* of Monday April 14th:

ATTACK NO. 7 BY RAPIST

> The rapist struck again in Cambridge early yesterday. Hooded and dressed from head to foot in black leather, he claimed his sixth victim in a bed-sitter off Hills Road... His latest victim, a 23-year-old girl, lay bound and gagged for six hours before managing to get to a window and raise the alarm.

Gail G. was a receptionist, not a student. She shared the house in Marshall Road with three other girls, but they had gone away for the weekend, and this was the first time she had been alone there. The flat was only 150 yards from Homerton College, scene of the rapist's fourth attack, which took place five months earlier, to the day. What's more, the new rape occurred exactly four months — to the hour! — after the previous one. The newspaper reported that he broke in through a back window, forcing the bolt from its mountings. The police thought that the attack took place sometime between 2 a.m. and 3.30 a.m. — "the girl was too confused to give them an exact time."

According to her own account:

"Somewhere about 10.30 p.m. I got undressed for the night and put on my blue night dress. It reached my knees and had wide shoulder-straps and a square neck-opening with lace in the same colour. The curtains were fully drawn. I'd already done that when it got dark. It was in my mind to run through the house to see if I'd remembered to lock up. I was sure the front door was fastened with its Yale lock as usual. Also the kitchen door was securely locked, with both the master key and an extra bolt. I didn't check the windows, either in the kitchen or bathroom or dining room.

The door to the bedroom was closed and the hook was in the loop in the door-frame, but I never lock it. Both windows were also fastened before I went to bed. I quickly went to sleep, but suddenly I woke up. I may have dreamt or felt in a dream that there was something wrong. There was, as the door was open. I got up at once, and became dreadfully scared when I saw that the door really was half-open — the hook attachment would allow it to come open, so I shut it. I knew for certain that I'd fully closed it before I went to bed. I got the keys and locked the door. I took the key out of the lock after I'd turned it fully round. Now I knew I was in safety, but I was nevertheless very shaken, and was still very frightened because I knew there was someone there. If it was a burglar, I hoped he would go away.

I tried to switch on the main bedroom light, but it wouldn't work, and that made me even more panicky. It was impossible for me to go to bed. I stayed sitting on the edge of the bed and listened intently. Ten minutes later I saw a flash of light, like from an electric torch. A cone of light sort of shone on the edge of the door and round the lock. Then it appeared outside on the windows, then back to the door, then the windows, and eventually came back to the lock. I was seized by terror — frantic terror. I knew I was alone in the house. I crept down into the bed as if to bury myself in it, hide myself from the invisible danger that was now threatening me.

I realised that, whoever he was, he was creeping around and first lighting up the door to my room, and then my window. He must have opened the front door. Otherwise he couldn't, as far as I could see, get to and fro so quickly. I heard this mysterious person go upstairs to another girl's room, Venetia, who was away. And then the light came back to my lock and shone directly through the keyhole in line with my bed.

There was a knock on the door. The handle was slowly being turned. I never said a word, hardly dared to breathe, just hoped whoever it was would go away. Suddenly there was an almighty bang, the door flew open, and this man was standing at the end of my bed, shining the torch right in my face. He asked me for money and I told him I had £15. Then he said, 'Turn onto your stomach.' I obeyed, as I was terror-stricken. He tied my arms and hands behind my back with my tights, which were lying on the chair at the side of the bed. 'Do you know who I am?, he asked. 'I'm the bloke they call the Cambridge Rapist. I'm the Rapist.' He put the covers over my head, but I could make out that the light had now come on again, and I heard him rummaging in my wardrobe and in the writing desk.

Then he took the covers off me again. The room looked as if a hurricane had been through it. Clothes lay scattered over the whole floor. My handbag was ransacked. All the drawers were emptied and just thrown onto the floor. My printed pink dress, which had been hanging on the back of the door was draped over the bedside lamp.

Now I saw him for the first time. Quite distinctly. He wasn't very big, around 5 ft 4 ins. Strongly built — at any rate, not thin. He was dressed from head to foot in black leather. A short black leather jacket that was tight-fitting. Very ordinary, with a zip fastener the whole way up, and side pockets. The zip wasn't fully done up, and I glimpsed a grey-green sweater. He had black leather gloves and, I think, black leather trousers. Round his neck he had a piece of steel cable or wire. His head was fully covered by a black leather mask, with cut-out holes for the eyes, and a zip that looked like an obscene mouth. The zip was silver or chrome. The mask was of smooth hide, and it seemed to me that the whole costume and mask were of the same quality.

The mask only reached down to his chin, and just below the chin I could see a gingery brown beard and he kept stroking it for a long time as if he wanted me to notice it, but it was matted and either hadn't been washed or it was false. Then he took a knife from the right pocket of the jacket — it was a dagger-type knife about seven inches long. I was now lying on my back. He sort of brushed the knife edge against my throat and said, 'If you scream I'll slit your throat.'

He knelt down over me, with his head turned towards me. With the knife he quickly cut the straps of my night dress from inside to out. It happened so quickly that I got a chilling sensation that the knife must be fantastically sharp. Then he ripped the nightie wide open at the front, brutally pulled me over on one side and pulled it from my back, tearing the pieces off and throwing them on the floor. I was now completely naked. He didn't say a word while he was undressing me like this, but then he asked, 'Why didn't you scream? You're very cooperative, aren't you?'

He stuck a cloth in my mouth. It smelt and tasted of oil. I clamped my mouth shut, but he succeeded in getting the cloth right in behind my teeth, and then he tied my mouth with something I later discovered was a pair of my tights. He got off me, went over to the door, and opened it out into the corridor. There was light out there. He stuck a shoe in the doorway to hold it open. Otherwise it's fixed to close itself. Then he took his trousers off, crawled onto me, and started mauling me. He rubbed and chafed my breasts and kissed them, while he whispered, 'Do you like that? Are you all right?' Quite incredibly grotesque! Obviously I couldn't reply as I was gagged both with a cloth and with tights.

Every time he spoke he opened the zip of his hood mouthpiece, and when he had finished he closed it again. He forced my legs apart. I still lay on my back. He held my shoulders down on the mattress. Then he stuck his penis into me. With his mouth near me, he said, 'Have you ever had sex before?' and then 'It's nice, isn't it? Does that hurt? Am I hurting you?' and 'Are you sure you're all right?' He moved to and fro on my body. The whole act of intercourse lasted a few minutes. I'm not even sure if he came. Then he got off me. He stood on the floor, leaned over me and whispered, 'Where is the other girl?' He took the gag from my mouth and asked me to answer him. He hadn't put his trousers on again yet.

He asked my name and I lied and said 'Lesley', and lied again about my surname, which I said was 'Applin' which I invented. He also asked how old I was and where I worked, and I said the Prudential, which was untrue, and that I was a cashier. He said, 'Good, you can get me some money, then.' Then he stuck the gag back into my mouth again, and then he also tied my feet round the ankles and my hands behind my back, so it was impossible for me to move. He asked me how I wanted to lie and I said on my back, and he then folded the sheet and blanket over me and made sure the bed was tidy. He was saying things like, 'You can't believe what you read in the papers. I don't really hurt people.' He asked repeatedly if I was lying comfortably, and then said 'Now you won't report me to the police.' I answered, 'No,' for safety's sake.

He went out, and it turned out later that my £15 were still in my purse. He picked up something which sounded like a plastic carrier bag from the hall, and left by the front door which he slammed.

Judging from the way he spoke and moved, I think he was in his forties. His clothes smelled musty, and he smelled dirty and unwashed. A smell of old tobacco-smoke or maybe factory smoke. When he kissed my breasts he pulled the zip in the mask to one side every time, and then closed it again.

I lay there for about two hours until it got light and managed to remove the dirty gag from my mouth with my tongue. With the help of the wall I managed to stand up and tried to move the window-catch with my teeth. I couldn't, so I moved to the dressing table, picked up a perfume bottle with my teeth and used this to move the catch. I opened the window from the top with my teeth, and then tried the bread knife from the kitchen to cut my bonds, but I didn't succeed. It was about 8.30 a.m. when the man from next door came out of the house, and I attracted his attention, and he told the girl living in that house who climbed through the window and freed me."

The brief newspaper account mentioned that after making a statement to the police and undergoing medical tests, the girl left to stay with relatives on the outskirts of Cambridge. Police questioned householders in the area, but no one saw or heard anything. As DS Hotson said to the reporter, "There is no magical method of wrapping this up. It is simply back to the hard slog of routine inquiries. We need the information from the public — because there is no doubt that somebody knows this man."

It was pointed out that the rapist was probably not worried by the lights in the room because of his new disguise, especially the skin-tight leather hood with eye slits and the zip-fastener mouth. However, no mention was made in the newspaper report of the most vital piece of new evidence — Gail's assessment that the man was in his forties. This turned out to be perfectly accurate, in stark contrast to the estimates by earlier victims. How was she able to get the age right despite him being far more covered up than on earlier occasions? One can only assume that she got a better look because the rape did not take place in darkness.

That same day, an important article appeared in the *Cambridge Evening News*, under the byline of Fulton Gillespie for the first time, entitled "He could be Dawn Raider". It revealed that the rumours I had been hearing for months were true, and that the police knew of at least three attempts to get at girls living alone since the rape of December 15th. So much for the wishful thinking of the many who wanted to believe that he had gone: "While the public thought that he had given up his campaign of terror, the police knew otherwise. They had had reports of telephone wires and lighting circuits being cut in bed-sitters in various parts of the city, but they made no official statements about it in the hope of catching their man." It is hard to understand the rationale behind this policy, especially since, as I was well aware myself, after a couple of months had passed, growing numbers of girls were starting to become complacent and had lowered their guard.

"Stories that he had left the district have always been discounted by the police — because they knew from his unsuccessful attempts that he was still active. Since the last rape on December 15, they have had reports of mysterious lipstick marks on windows, the tell-tale phone and lighting circuit cuts and girls reporting 'noises' in the night either inside or outside their flats."

(In fact it was subsequently reported in the *Sunday Telegraph* of May 11th that on the night of the Marshall Road rape the rapist was known to have written in lipstick on the window of another house in the road shared by three girl students of Homerton "Sleep tight — the Rapist"). I have always found it extremely puzzling that the police did not issue alerts to warn girls that the rapist was still active, instead of letting them grow complacent, but when I asked Bernard Hotson about this point recently he told me that it could have been counter-productive at that time to give publicity to graffiti.

After the rapist's trial and sentencing, the police revealed that he had told them of a whole series of "visits" to houses during this period, but without rapes: four houses on January 27th (22 Marshall Road, 205 Hills Road, 117 Richmond Road, 114 Huntingdon Road), three on February 3rd (32 Rock Road, 10 Blinco Grove, 89 Hartington Grove), one on March 17th (12a Springfield Road), two on March 23rd (36 Eltisley Avenue, 11 Marlowe Road), two on April 12th (22 Marshall Road, 10 Blinco Grove). After the Marshall Road rape of April 13th, there were other "visits" — two on May 4th (16 Madingley Road, 57 Storey's Way), and one on May 5th (5 Pye Terrace).

We now learned that a criminal whom the police had dubbed the "Dawn Raider" — a petty thief who expertly breaks into houses stealing only cash — had been operating since October 1974 in the same area chosen by the rapist. "They have not discounted the possibility that they may be one and the same person. The Dawn Raider strikes between two and four in the morning, thus keeping the same hours as the rapist. He also uses the same expert method of getting in — skilfully and silently opening windows and back doors; and he is reckoned to be wiry and short like the rapist because he has been able to get through windows which men of average build could not."

The latest rape had occurred in Marshall Road, and the Raider too had once visited that road, breaking into a different house. In addition, the rapist's hood and wigs were reminiscent of the fact that the Raider once lost a fur hat after breaking into a house near Neville Road, a stone's throw from where the new rape took place — it had been whipped off his head by a clothes line as he escaped through a back garden, the same escape route sometimes used by the rapist.

Gillespie described the determination of the police to get their man, the thousands of man-hours already devoted to the task, the checking of every imaginable lead; but so far they had lacked that vital ingredient, the element of luck: "They have had no breaks at all." Their man apparently has no "form" (a previous criminal record); he has not been seen and so cannot be identified by his victims; he leaves nothing to chance, planning his attacks with meticulous care, and there are no fingerprints. He is not even known to local criminals. He probably does not drink (no girl has yet reported smelling alcohol) and "he probably lives alone or with an elderly mother."

Without a lucky break, such as the man picking the wrong flat and being overpowered, or being caught on the way to or from a raid, police have little left to go on. "They feel their situation acutely. They know the public are asking the awful question: 'Why can't you get this man?'" But without information from the public they were largely helpless. As DCS Naan was quoted as saying, "Anyone knowing this man, or anyone who even suspects they know of such a man and who does not tell the police is vicariously responsible for what he has done."

The latest rape was also widely reported in the national press, with some inevitable errors creeping in thanks to sloppy journalism. For example, it was claimed in several papers that the rapist wore a "black Ku Klux-Klan-type" disguise. It was said that the first girl to be raped was "dragged from her bath", and that the girl in the unsuccessful attack had beaten him off with the hot iron. One tabloid revealed that the victims had received clinical help and medical treatment to ensure they do not become pregnant. Some had wanted to move away from Cambridge; all were afraid of it happening again, and did not want their names published.

The *Daily Mail* quoted a "blond undergraduate" as saying; "We had hoped he might somehow have gone away. It's rather unpleasant to come back at the end of vacation and find that this is still going on." Another girl spoke of the "edgy jokes" that were going round college, and the nervousness of the women of the town. For the female students returning to their colleges, it was the beginning of another term of worry, but not hysteria.

According to Dr Janet Harket, deputy head of Girton College: "We have taken quite a lot of precautions. Extra porters patrol the college grounds and visitors are signed in and have to identify themselves. The two other girl colleges, New Hall and Newnham, have taken similar steps."

Interviewed by the *Daily Mail* (April 15th), DS Hotson revealed the clear mental picture of the rapist which he had formed, and did not mince his words: "He is a frightened little bastard. He must operate at night to give himself nerve. For the same reason he must carry a knife to terrify his victims. He is careful to pick only houses where he thinks he will find girls living on their own… Nothing suggests he even knows the names of his victims. They say he talks a lot but that he does not give anything away, no clue to his identity."

It was estimated that there were about 30,000 young bachelor girls in Cambridge at this time, living alone in bedsitters away from the protection of colleges. However, thanks to DS Hotson's recommendation, some of these girls were no longer alone at night, and this led the rapist to a bad choice of house for his next attack.

Detective Superintendent Bernard Hotson

Chapter 9
The eighth and ninth attacks

Early on a Sunday morning, May 4th, the rapist struck a college hostel housing nine girls, unaware that one of them had her boyfriend spending the night. The next day the *Cambridge Evening News* had the following encouraging headline:

RAPIST FOILED IN ATTEMPT AT CITY HOSTEL

The Cambridge rapist, wearing his now notorious black leather hood, made three unsuccessful attempts early yesterday to get at nine girls asleep in a college hostel in the city. But he was foiled by the girls' security measures. All interior doors downstairs had been bolted. His frantic attempts to smash open a back door woke one girl who alerted the others.

The attack took place on an isolated New Hall hostel, off Madingley Road, at 3.35 a.m. It was one of several run by the college for its female students, and was several hundred yards from the main road. The rapist had first tried to break in through a small lattice window by the main door, but once inside he was confronted by a locked interior door which he attempted to force, but in vain.

He then went back outside, and tried another window before making his third attempt by smashing the glass in the back door to reach the Yale lock inside. He managed to open this door, but then found himself in the kitchen, which had doors leading to the main part of the hostel, but these were all locked and bolted. The clumsy breaking of the glass woke one of the girls, and when the lights came on he fled — but not before three of the girls had seen him.

They described him to police as being "very small and thin". They saw he was wearing his black leather hood with eye slits and zip-fastener mouth-opening plus a heavy blue anorak.

One of the girls had her boyfriend staying the night in a separate part of the house, and, as luck would have it, he was a friend of mine, a fellow archaeology student, James Monnington. Now a successful lawyer in Southampton, he well remembers that night, and has provided the following account:

"In the spring of 1975 I had graduated but remained in Cambridge with my girlfriend who was in her final year at New Hall which is on the Huntingdon Road. It was an all women college at that time, and they had a residence behind the college where my girlfriend had a room. There were probably about eight or ten students there and there was no warden. In term time I managed to live in her room without notice from the authorities or complaint from the other girls. Indeed because of the activities of the Cambridge rapist my presence was rather welcomed.

The residence lay between the Madingley Road and the Huntingdon Road and was set in substantial grounds. The garden to the front on the Madingley Road side must have been some 150 to 200 yards long, with a lawn and vegetable garden at the bottom. A hedge ran around the perimeter and it was very secluded. To the rear there was a narrow path running through thick vegetation which led up to New Hall. The path was unlit until one got near to the college buildings.

The activities of the rapist sent waves of anxiety through the town and the girls' residence was a sensitive barometer. After each attack the tension level would rise and then begin to fade as the weeks passed. Then it would again rise sharply after another incident. Overall there was an underlying sense of anxiety and hyper-vigilance.

On the day before the rapist's entry into the residence a man was seen in the vegetable garden. In normal circumstances this would probably not have caused comment, but the sighting caused alarm amongst some of the girls and I believe the police might have been notified.

The students' residence had a front door leading into a hallway, at one end of which was a large kitchen. The hallway was separated from the kitchen by an internal door which could be locked. There was a back door into the kitchen and a back staircase leading from the kitchen to the upstairs bedrooms. There was another door at the top of these backstairs which could also be locked.

My girlfriend's room was downstairs and accessed from the corridor, and was adjacent to the kitchen. In the early hours of the morning there was a tremendous commotion with one of the girls running down the stairs and screaming. We got up feeling dazed from sleep but soon realised that there had been an intrusion. Clearly the intruder had been disturbed and we soon found the evidence of the efforts that had been made to get in.

The front door showed evidence of being forced but was still locked. However, the intruder had got into the kitchen by forcing the back door and had then made efforts to get into the upstairs by the back staircase. However, the door at the top of the stairs had been locked, and he had failed. The intruder had then begun to gouge out the lock from the timber of the locked door between the kitchen and the corridor, but had been disturbed. This door was probably only a couple of feet the other side of the bedroom wall from where I was sleeping.

Someone tried phoning '999' from the house phone. The line had been cut. As the only male, I was despatched (or perhaps I felt obliged) to go and phone from a call box or the college. I ran up the dark pathway towards New Hall, the path edged by thick vegetation on either side. I anticipated being 'jumped' at any moment and was thoroughly afraid. I found a call box on the Huntingdon Road and dialled '999' and spluttered pretty incoherently about the rapist until the call handler managed to get sufficient detail of location to send the police.

The police arrived and examined the scene and took details. The local press came the next morning and I gave a very bad interview, being concerned mainly about my illicit living in the female residence.

What I do remember clearly is that one of the students, who was of resilient disposition, had been out quite late in the evening and had come back through the kitchen door and up the back stairs. She admitted that she had almost forgotten to lock the door at the top of the stairs. If she had left it open then the intruder would have gained access into the upstairs bedrooms and the scenario could have ended very differently...a rape...a 'citizen's arrest'...? it was only the vigilance of the students in locking the internal doors that had prevented him having access.

Several of the girls remained very shaken by the incident for some considerable while and there was palpable relief when the rapist was subsequently arrested."

****

It was James who discovered that the telephone wires had been cut, a normal part of the rapist's modus operandi. Presumably he had not bothered to cut the light circuit because, as in the previous attack, he felt that the hood ensured that he could not be recognised, so the lights were irrelevant. By the time James was able to call the police, the rapist had made good his escape. Police set up road blocks, and brought in dogs, but drew a blank.

Surprisingly, DS Hotson announced to the press that he was not certain that this was the work of the rapist rather than just a burglar: "There are certain things about this which lead me to believe that this may not in fact be connected with the rapist", but he was unwilling to say what those "certain things" were; and when I asked him about this point recently, he could not recall what he had been referring to. The girls, for their part, were quite sure they had seen the rapist. A week later, the press reported that he had stolen a notice from the back door which said "Keep locked to deter the Rapist."

The day after the first newspaper report, I was able to speak to James and his girlfriend about the incident. They informed me that the newspaper report was quite inaccurate in parts, since only one girl had actually seen the man, who was "very small and weedy", and only from behind. They said that about eighty-five police had arrived, together with dogs, and that the hostel became "like Fort Knox".

Just as in mid-December the rapist had apparently been so furious at being thwarted at one house that he immediately attacked another, so this time too his frustration seems to have caused him to seek another victim shortly afterwards. Only two days later, on Tuesday May 6th, he struck — and for the first time in broad daylight, thus changing the pattern of his previous behaviour completely. He selected an area close to a Pye Electronics factory.

That same day, the evening paper carried a huge and horrifying headline:

CITY RAPE DRAMA IN DAYLIGHT

Girl No. 8 stabbed in lunchtime attack

A girl was raped and stabbed this afternoon in the Cambridge rapist's most vicious attack of his seven month reign of terror in the city. For the first time he struck in broad daylight at a terraced house in Chesterton. His victim was a secretary in her early twenties. He attacked about 1 p.m. as Pye workers streamed along Church Street. He struck at a house at the end of Pye Terrace. His victim was taken to Addenbrooke's Hospital where surgeons were carrying out an emergency abdominal operation. A hospital spokesman said the girl's condition was "satisfactory".

A girl who lived next door at No. 4 said she had heard rumbling noises, but saw nothing: "I just took it to be someone moving around the house." Neighbours said that they understood the rapist had lain in wait. The girl had gone home for lunch — ironically, something she had never done before — and was alone in the house. Like the other victims, she had been bound and gagged, so that it was some time before she was able to raise the alarm, thus enabling the rapist to escape. Police were alerted by ambulance men who were called to the house by the girl herself around 1 p.m. Road blocks were immediately set up, and police converged on the area, stopping, searching and questioning all men around 5 ft 5 ins. in height. Several were taken to Parkside police headquarters for further questioning.

The newspaper reported that this time the rapist had been wearing a brown anorak, according to the girl. Police said that she had been fully clothed when she was surprised by the rapist. He cut off her clothes with the sharp double-edged knife he always carried. DS Hotson stated that "We cannot say as yet how she came to be stabbed. We do not know whether it was in a struggle or whether she was simply attacked with the knife." The wound was three-quarters of an inch deep, and had penetrated the wall of the abdomen.

All was later revealed in the statement made to police by the girl, Amanda H., after her operation. She had been away for the weekend, and arrived in Cambridge at 11.45 a.m., took the 12.05 p.m. bus to Chesterton and was home by 12.25 p.m.

"No one knew I was coming home at that time of that day. I stood for a moment in the hall to collect my thoughts. I scribbled down a few things I had to do — shopping, banal things for the household — and was making the list with my back to the door. I suddenly became aware of someone standing behind me. I turned round to see a man in my bedroom only a few feet away. He was not much over 5 ft 4 ins. Slight, he seemed to me, with a khaki-coloured anorak with a zip. Black or very dark-brown trousers with a zip in front. He wore a black leather hood that covered his whole head. It looked particularly horrible with two holes crudely cut out for the eyes. His eyes were blue. I guessed he was in his twenties. I don't know if it had a zip for the mouth, but running across the forehead was the word RAPIST. It was painted on, maybe with white colour, or maybe it was white letters that were stitched to the hood.

I was absolutely shocked. Sort of frozen to the spot. And at first I could barely realise that he was speaking to me. He grabbed hold of me and I started to struggle to get to the door. I noticed a knife in his right hand. The handle of the knife had string or a piece of wire attached to it and this was tied to his wrist.

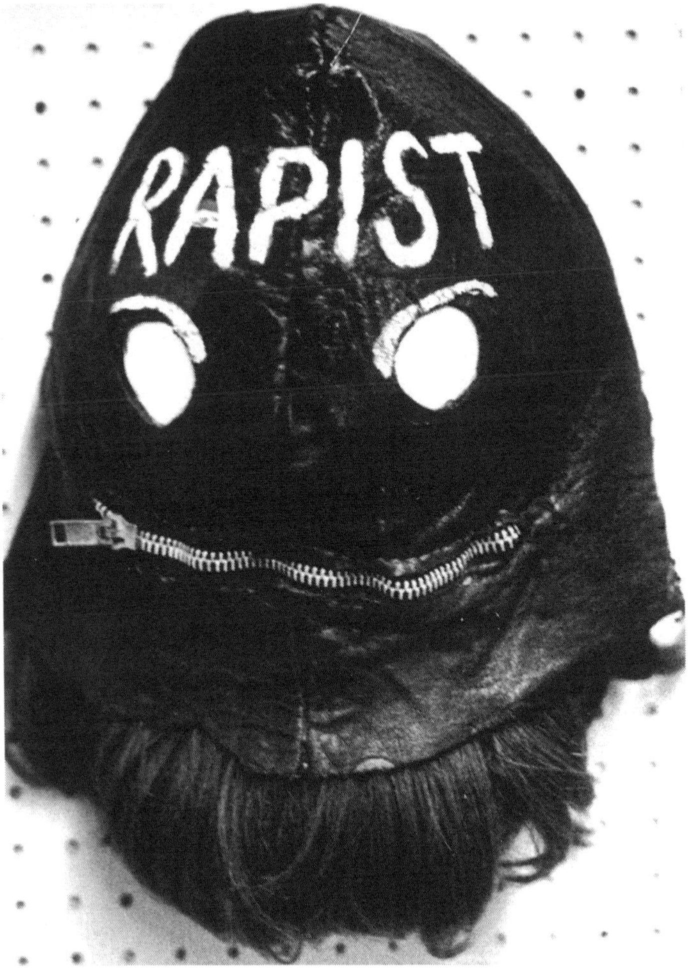
RAPIST

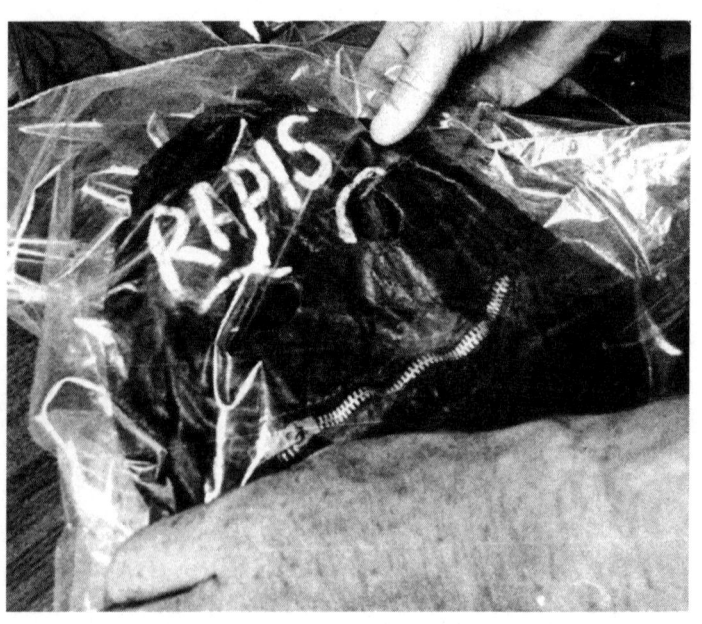

'If you don't keep still I'll put the knife through you,' he said. 'I've come to rape you. To rape you, do you hear?' And I remember him putting the knife to the right side of my stomach and although he only pricked me and didn't penetrate very far it started to bleed immediately. It must have been very pointed and sharp. I begged him to take what I had in the way of money and valuables — 'You can have anything you like if you leave me alone,' I said.

'My friend is coming at one o'clock,' I said, but this didn't seem to have any effect on him. He ordered me: 'Put your hands behind your back,' in a commanding voice. 'Get on the floor. Lie down. You're talking too much. I hate you.' He knocked me down and tied my hands and arms behind my back with a pair of tights and when I managed to get them free he pulled the flex from the bedside lamp and secured my wrists. I was defenceless. 'You're talking too much,' he said again, and stuffed one end of a yellow and white towel in my mouth and seemed amazed it kept falling out. He then pushed me into the front bedroom, and tied the gag in place with a pair of tights. He brought my radio in with him, threw it to the floor and smashed it.

He started to tear my clothes off — long black cotton trousers, a green V-necked short-sleeved knitted jumper, black tights, black and white bra and panties. He took out his penis, but it wasn't fully stiff and he could only push it a bit up me. He squeezed my breasts a few times. Still with his gloves on. He messed around, I suppose, for half an hour, and I'm not sure if he came at all. Then he talked: 'Richard screws you, doesn't he?' (I had told him that I was expecting my boyfriend, Richard). 'He comes here,' I said and asked him, 'What if I get pregnant?' 'I hope you do,' he said. Three or four minutes after he went, I got the kitchen knife to cut myself free, dressed in fresh clothes, and went to the phone box 200 yards away in Chesterton High Street to call the police and ambulance.

There was a wound in the right side of my stomach, four cuts on the palms of my hands and thumb, and scratches and bruises on both wrists. I have thought about it a lot and I am of the opinion that he got more satisfaction through seeing me frightened and terrified of being tied up than the actual act of sexual intercourse. He spent most of his time tying me up and pushing me about and wanting to be boss, and the sexual intercourse seemed to be secondary to the attack. I suppose it was the sight of my fear and the knowledge that he had me in his power."

One can trace the rapist's growing sense of self-importance. During the third rape, at Homerton, he had referred to himself as the "Raper". During the sixth rape in April, presumably taking his cue from the newspaper description on December 9th, he called himself "The Cambridge Rapist". And now, finally, he had proudly placed the word on his mask. This truly macabre embellishment has come to epitomise the case, and will always be associated with the Cambridge Rapist, even though it was only worn during this last successful attack.

The daylight attack brought some fresh clues which were to prove of enormous importance, even though, once again, the victim and other local residents were very mistaken about her assailant's age. The very next day, the *Cambridge Evening News* announced, after questioning dozens of people in the area of Pye Terrace and Church Street, Chesterton, that a man had been seen just before the rape, riding a bicycle up and down the street. He was described as young, probably in his twenties, wearing a tan coloured anorak or windcheater, and dark trousers. He was thought to be wearing a fair or light brown cheap wig, dark glasses with steel rims and had what witnesses described as "an unnaturally tanned complexion", probably due to make-up, and a fleshy face. A third photofit of this individual was promptly published — but once again, it bore no resemblance to the rapist.

However, the truly crucial clue that emerged from the locals' testimony was that this man was riding an old black bicycle that rattled. And a second piece of information revealed by the police was that they believed the man had entered and left through the front door, to which he had a duplicate Yale key.

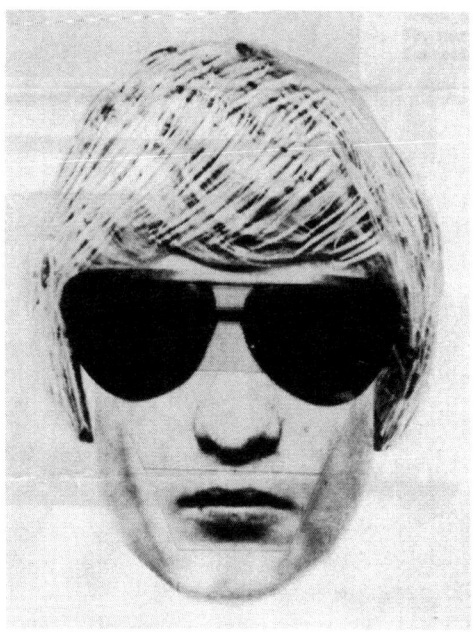

The third police photofit

One positive aspect of the daylight attack was that it enabled the police to eliminate a number of suspects from their list, since they had solid alibis for that time of day.

On May 8th, the *Cambridge Evening News'* chief reporter, Fulton Gillespie, disclosed a new twist to the latest attack. It seems that while the rapist was attacking Amanda in the house, her flatmate was at the police station reporting a break-in the night before, by the rapist. She had found a bathroom window slightly open. It seems he had been in to reconnoitre and plan the attack for the next day. Not only was it the first time that Amanda had been in the house at lunchtime, it was the first time that her flatmate — a 20-year-old dark-haired secretary — had not, because she was at the station. Had she gone home as usual she could have walked in and been attacked herself. Amanda, of course, having been away for the weekend, knew nothing about the break-in — her flatmate was planning to tell her that night when she got home from work.

The police issued a further appeal for information, claiming they were fairly sure that the rapist lived alone in a room or flat, and thus they called on all landlords and landladies and letting agencies to check their files to see if any of their properties was occupied by a small man in his twenties. They appealed to tenants to get to know their neighbours, on the basis that many people renting accommodation have no idea who lives in the flat next door or upstairs. They also set up a direct "Rapeline" telephone link to Cambridge police HQ, manned 24 hours a day, for anyone with information. Callers were told they could remain anonymous.

Once again, the national press also had a field day with the new rape, using terms like "demon rapist", "hooded rapist", and "the kinky pint-sized Cambridge rapist". There were the usual inaccuracies — for example, several tabloids claimed that the rapist had stabbed her and tied her up after the rape, and one stated that all his rapes had occurred in the Chesterton area. Surprisingly, only the *Daily Express* got hold of the news that the hood now had the word "RAPIST" on it. It was revealed that more than 8000 people in Cambridge had been interviewed so far, and thirty-five "positive suspects" had been cleared.

DS Hotson's latest theory was that "this man is a resident of Cambridge who has a valid reason for being away from the city for long periods which would account for the gaps of time between the attacks. He is also a man with a thorough knowledge of the bedsitter area. This man obviously hates women. His hatred comes over in his conversations. He has no self-confidence like ordinary men. He cannot have a proper relationship or make friends with a woman. His real thrill doesn't come from the sex. It seems he is sexually inadequate. This man is a nutter. He's sick and dangerous."

A few days later, and quite prophetically, he declared: "Luck is never completely one-sided. Higher justice will ensure that this man's luck will run out eventually." It was fervently hoped that this would happen before there was another attack, because the escalation of the rapist's violence made everyone worry that the next victim might be killed.

Chapter 10
The Bodyguard Service

As always, I had been following events with keen interest, and it was at this point that I had my one genuine insight into the case. The rapist was obviously well aware that the police, and indeed the public in general, were actively seeking a small man on a bicycle. He could do nothing about his height. But what if he were dressing as a woman? Nobody was looking for a woman at all, and he had already shown that he had a wide range of wigs and disguises at his disposal. I well remember mentioning this theory to my friend in the archaeology department, but I have no idea if he thought it worth passing on to his son in the police force.

On May 8th, the *Cambridge Evening News* on its front page offered a £1000 reward for information leading to the arrest and subsequent conviction of the rapist, while a Cambridge businessman, John Carlin, managing director of C and M Plasterers Ltd, likewise offered a £250 reward, saying, "I feel very strongly about this. I think the only way we are going to get this animal is to put up some substantial reward" (a second businessman, Charles Ronayne, managing director of Damp and Decay Control Ltd, likewise offered £250 a week later). The *Cambridge Evening News* also issued, for the first time, a poster featuring the third, latest photofit of the disguised man seen on a bicycle. It was reported that the new confidential hotline to the rape incident room had been jammed with calls, and police had been given the names of hundreds of men, mostly by women wishing to remain anonymous, but DS Hotson stated that so far there had been no new developments.

The city's MP, David Lane, made a TV appeal to the rapist's mother that, if she was aware of her son's activities, she should tell the police. This was, of course, based on the belief that he lived entirely on his own or was being shielded by a mother who knew his terrible secret. A week later, DCS Charles Naan, still in overall charge of the case, likewise appealed on television for the rapist to give himself up, while a separate appeal was made by a psychiatrist who said, "I think I know how you feel inside. I think you are getting desperate. I think you have got this sort of irresistible impulse that is getting worse. I am afraid you may be planning some final dramatic tragedy in the hope that somehow this is all going to make it go away. But it won't, it will only make things very much worse." He asked the rapist to contact him through the Samaritans and talk to him on the telephone. The result of this appeal was later revealed at the trial.

DS Hotson gave an interview to Fulton Gillespie of the *Cambridge Evening News* which appeared on May 9th. Gillespie wrote: "He knows at the end of the day that seven girls have had their bodies defiled and their minds tainted by the cowardly attacks of one single, solitary, vile little animal who has to carry a knife to be somebody — and Det. Supt. Bernard Hotson has so far failed to catch him." He reported that Hotson "has a daughter himself. She is the right age, but she does not live in Cambridge. But even that offers him little comfort... I think of the seven girls first, I think of all the other girls in this city living in holy terror, and I think of the parents, perhaps worried sick somewhere up in Huddersfield or wherever, and then I think: 'Have I missed something? Is something not in place? What have I not done that I could have done? Are we covering all angles?'"

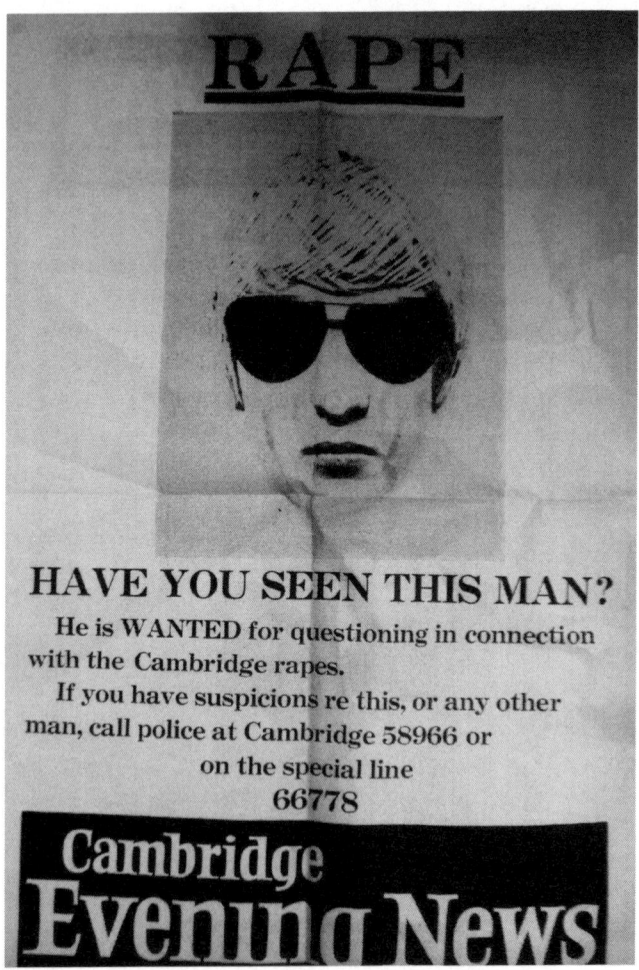

Poster published by *The Cambridge Evening News* and displayed around the City

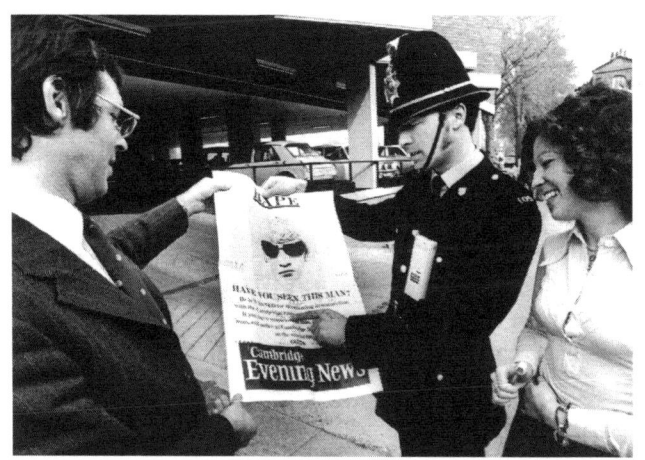

In a more revealing interview given to Lynda Lee-Potter in the *Daily Mail* of May 8th, his fatigue and frustration were apparent (he told another newspaper, "I'm 49 and I feel 94"). He looked exhausted, had had only a cup of black coffee at breakfast, and was working 20 hours a day, seven days a week. "One sees one's wife briefly at breakfast. There was no Christmas. I go to bed in the early hours of the morning, sleep with one ear on the telephone, my eyes open as the sun rises." With regard to the victims, he said, "The scars on the bodies of these girls will heal. The scars on their minds will never heal. They are good girls. They are hard-working pleasant, nice girls. They are all good girls", he re-emphasised angrily. "Not one of these girls asked for it or provoked it. They were in their own homes, alone, and thought they were safe."

Turning to the rapist himself, he said, "He knows more than we do. All the cards are in his hand. He picks the place, he changes the pattern at the drop of a hat. He's done his research, he knows Cambridge very, very well. This man is different from the majority. He operates indoors, he operates to a plan. It's not the raping, it's the terrorising that makes this man so dangerous. The black leather mask he wears is associated with the extreme fringe of certain sexual deviants. Before he operated in the dark, now he's picked the daytime. It may be a way of saying to us, 'Look how clever I am.' With most rapists there is a pattern, a continuity. This man has none. He dislikes the girls; his motive is his dislike. He has shown no compassion, no hint of kindness to any of his victims."

A psychiatrist told the journalist that "He could well be impotent without his mask or if the girl were to see his face. With the mask he feels powerful, he feels the master, he needs to feel the girl is frightened of him, it heightens his sexual pleasure. This sort of behaviour invariably hides an inadequate personality with basically a low threshold of confidence. It would not be over-dramatic to assume these experiences could permanently prevent these girls ever forming a stable physical relationship with a loving man." One hopes that this last speculation proved to be wrong in every case.

The *Guardian* of May 8th focused on the intensified security arrangements being adopted all over Cambridge. Newnham College had hired extra staff to man the porters' lodge day and night. The thirty girls living outside the college had been warned to lock themselves in. For once, the undergraduates were welcoming the college's motherly interference. Taxi firms recorded a major increase in girls using cabs at night, and asking the drivers to escort them right into their flats to make sure no one was inside. Working girls living in bedsits were particularly anxious, and hardware stores reported that sales of locks, chains and window catches had shot up. Windows were being booby-trapped with empty bottles. Girls kept whistles, buzzers, aerosols, pepper, heavy torches, knives, scissors, clubs, hammers or pokers by their beds. Self-defence demonstrations were given. Some women said that their boyfriends had become more solicitous and now saw them home instead of leaving them at the bus stop. "Life is difficult in Cambridge just now for men who are less than about 5ft 6in tall. Most girls are wary of short strangers and the police held twelve short men in custody overnight on Tuesday."

And yet the *Daily Telegraph* of the same day reported that, despite police appeals, many girls in Cambridge had refused to heed advice for their safety. "The local evening newspaper regularly carries advertisements for accommodation to let. A few days ago, one of these ran: 'Third professional girl, 20-25, for house, own room...' and then went on to give the full address in Cambridge." Interestingly, it also revealed for the first time that "tests on clothing coupled with medical examinations of the victims have produced two vital clues. One was the rapist's blood group, and the other was a physical characteristic which is of such significance that the police have asked for it to be kept secret."

Such was the impact of the Pye Terrace rape that, for the first time, there was talk in the local paper on May 10th of vigilante groups having been set up: "Vigilante patrols have been formed in some bed-sit areas of Cambridge by householders anxious to protect single girls from the rapist." In particular, some gangs of youths were roaming the streets of the Arbury council housing estate. However, such groups were not welcomed by the police. As DS Hotson put it, "I realise that these people are motivated by the best of intentions, but I must say that here we are not involved with a 90-minute Western television film. We do not want men wandering round the city at night armed with cricket stumps, looking for the rapist. This operation must be left to the police, for we are dealing with a cunning and highly dangerous man. Efforts of a few well-intentioned people at night could effectively nullify the police operation. I cannot go into any details, but I hope any group of people will not form patrols of this kind because it will mess up what we are trying to do."

By contrast DS Hotson greatly welcomed an initiative which had been announced in the *Cambridge Evening News* the day before. from my own college, Gonville and Caius. Richard Jopling, a 25-year-old post-graduate student, had come up with the idea of a "free student volunteer bodyguard service", whereby girls who were worried about being alone at night could telephone, and two bona fide students would go out to their flat or house, with sleeping bags, and sleep on a couch or the floor.

I was told a story at the time — which may have been apocryphal or embellished — that the scheme was first presented to a young police detective, who responded: "Lads, this is just the kind of initiative we have been hoping for. But I tell you what — let's keep it really secret, and then there is a much better chance that he'll attack a house without realising it has men inside, and we'll be able to catch him red handed." The students pointed out that, if the scheme was kept really secret, then no girls would know about it, to which the detective replied: "Hmm, yes, you've got a point there."

Richard Jopling

Be that as it may, it was announced that the scheme would operate every night, starting from 10 p.m. on May 10th onwards. According to Richard, "This is a genuine attempt to protect girls who are alone and frightened until such time as the rapist is caught. We have already got twenty or so students who will act as overnight escorts for any girls living alone. But we want more from all the other colleges. They must carry proper student identification, and all coming forward will be carefully vetted. If we don't like a guy he will be sent on his way. Two students will be assigned to any girl or group of girls living alone. They will need to bring their own sleeping bags, and they will sleep overnight in the hallway of the girls' flats. We will ensure that the two students assigned to the girls will be unknown to each other, simply to put any fears the girls may have out of their minds."

These guidelines were highly laudable but, as will be seen, as time went on and the novelty wore off, the modus operandi had to be altered in various ways. At the start, however, it was seen as a great occasion, and many of us gathered in the college MCR (Middle Combination Room, the lounge for graduates) that first evening to see how it would function. The *Cambridge Evening News* of May 10th had reported that "The scheme was announced yesterday and already there has been a big demand from the girls." As I noted in my diary, however, that first evening there were only three calls, and six students were sent out. I stayed chatting to Richard till 11 p.m., and offered my services for the future.

On the second night, once again, there were only three calls. We began to hear rumours that "Women's Libbers" were spreading the word that they did not want to be guarded by men, and preferred to have girls grouped together — "safety in numbers!" Eileen Phillips, president of Newnham Students' Union, told the *Sunday Telegraph* (May 11th) that members of the university women's groups were getting together to protect themselves: "There's a feeling in the women's movement that you don't want men to protect you." Groups of girls were preparing lists of addresses and telephone numbers so that anyone left alone in houses could go to stay with others at any time. On the other hand, Ann Carr, president of New Hall junior common room, thought differently: "If you've got a boyfriend he's bound to be worried. We certainly value the presence of a man in the house." However, as far as I can recall, very few — if any — girl students ever requested our services. It was always working girls in bedsits around the city who called us out.

On the third day (May 12th), the *Cambridge Evening News* printed a picture of Richard and some other students, and they were also featured on local BBC television. Perhaps as a result of this extra exposure, there were more calls that night — five! The paper also revealed that a clairvoyant from Worksop had been brought in by a Nottinghamshire newspaper. DS Hotson had met him and told him the present state of the investigations: "I am not sure what he had in mind, but he was not able to tell us any more than we already know." The clairvoyant then left the city, telling police he would be in touch after he had time to "think about things."

The *Daily Express* of May 18th said that a clairvoyant, Simon Alexander, had declared that the rapist may be vaguely known by one of his victims. He may also be connected with the university or education authority, has a scar or mark on his leg, and a throat or chest complaint. Having toured the scenes of the attacks and felt the "vibrations", he believes the wanted man has been interviewed by the police but not necessarily for rape. His hair is slightly receding and has been slicked down with oil. The man is slightly built but with a thick-featured face and lives in the north of the city. He predicted yesterday that the rapist would be caught in about a week's time, but there would be another attack before that. A Cambridge police spokesman said they had been "very impressed" with some of his information — he could not possibly have known some of the details just by reading the papers. Some of his information is known only to the police, the rapist and his victims. Obviously, we now know that much of this declaration was completely wrong, but Bernard Hotson does recall that the police were indeed impressed by some of the things which he said.

Meanwhile rapist scare stories cropped up frequently, and each and every one had to be checked out by the police. For example, the Chesterton area was sealed off one Saturday night after a small, fair-haired man was disturbed in the women's toilets of the Pye factory canteen during a staff dance. He answered the description of the cyclist seen before the Pye Terrace rape, and so police searched the grounds and surrounding area with dogs for an hour, but found nothing. Another story swept the Arbury estate when the rape squad had a score of calls one Friday to say that a young woman and an 8-year-old girl had been attacked; but neither the rapist nor these alleged victims were found. On May 16th, squads of rape-hunt detectives rushed to New Hall after a report that a man had been seen in the grounds, but a search with dogs revealed nothing.

The bodyguard scheme — described with tongue firmly in cheek by a friend of mine as "rent-a-thug" — appealed to the media, who were ever eager for a new angle on the saga. I remember that we were filmed for ITN's *News at Ten* on May 13th, and a group photograph of us was taken in the MCR on May 12th by the *Daily Express*; it later appeared (May 14th) under the embarrassing headline "Like knights of old, the bedroll brigade set out to save their maidens' honour". As I noted in my diary, after the bodyguards had gone off for the night, one of the photographers asked me to pretend (in the MCR!) to be sleeping outside a girl's door, but I refused. Shortly afterwards, a late telephone call came in from a girl who was very frightened; I took the call, but then her flatmate arrived, thus removing the need for students to go out to her.

On the evening of May 13th, when ITN filmed us, there were again five calls, and I went out to "do my duty" for the first time. As I had no bicycle, I got a lift from a friend to 37 Grantchester Street (just opposite Owlestone Road, scene of the fifth attack, and hence in "rapist territory") where I was to spend the night along with a diminutive Scottish student called Alan who, in accordance with the guidelines, was a complete stranger to me. My friend Jonathan, a veterinary student, had been with me in the MCR that evening, but had been sent out to a different address. Alan and I were to guard two girls, one of whom had two small children. We all chatted till midnight, and then Alan and I slept on spare mattresses. But I remember that it was very hard to fall asleep — because for the first time I was in a place which might well be attacked by the rapist, and it would then be down to Alan and me to confront him. But we had no weapons! I eventually nodded off, but

I had dreams of the rapist, and doing some rather unpleasant things to him. Fortunately, after that first night the feeling of apprehension passed, and I always slept soundly when "on duty".

The Bodyguard Squad, author 3rd from left

Other bodyguards reported similar feelings of anxiety and tension on their first nights. It was a new experience for all of us. One told a newspaper, "I was frightened and tense all night because this is no joke — the girls in this city are scared stiff." But one girl said, "It's very reassuring to have two hefty men sleeping in your lounge." Astonishingly, some of the girls who requested our services began by saying "I don't want to be a nuisance, but..!" Posters seeking male volunteers were circulated around all the colleges, which said: "Please help. What may be a slight inconvenience to you may be a life saver for some girl."

By May 17th, however, the novelty of the scheme had definitely worn off, and that night Richard was desperately seeking volunteers. I went out with a second-year Caius maths student called Colin to guard 16 Clare Street. It housed a girl with three small daughters. The eldest infant sized us up, and decided she liked me best, so I got a kiss. We watched TV till 1.30 a.m., and then I was given the spare bed while Colin worked through the night — it was exam time, of course. At least Colin had it easy — numerous girl students were suffering sleepless nights and constant anxiety, which threatened their examination prospects. Janet Moore, the senior tutor of New Hall told the press that police were patrolling the college grounds with dogs every night, and because girls felt more secure in college "we have used every last broom cupboard to accommodate them from outside. College staff are taking them into their homes — my own house is full — and where a girl needs a complete rest she is being sent outside of Cambridge."

On May 19th I reported for duty again — by this time the scheme had been extended and was being run from CSU (the Cambridge Students' Union) at 3 Round Church Street — this was a positive move, as the Caius MCR phone had often been engaged for long periods. A circular had been widely distributed:

****

CSU/CAIUS MCR RAPIST SECURITY SCHEME

To provide protection to anybody who wants it.

PLEASE READ THE FOLLOWING CAREFULLY

This joint scheme has two objectives:

A. To combine girls living alone or in small numbers with others in the same position to achieve safety in numbers.

B. To extend the scheme already put in operation by Caius MCR which enables anybody worried to phone for persons to come and spend the night in their home for protection.

A. COMBINATION SCHEME FOR WOMEN'S COLLEGES

a) If you are living alone or just in twos and would like to join someone else in a similar situation who has spare room for the duration of this term, then please apply to CSU as soon as possible.

b) If you have any spare room in your accommodation that could be used, and you would be prepared to let any girls living alone or in twos move in for any length of time up to the duration of this term then PLEASE contact CSU as soon as possible. Any offer of this sort will be a tremendous help to someone.

When applying ask for either Robert Breare or Pippa Berry. Every effort will be made to fit you or two of you into any available accommodation space that is offered.

B. DIAL-A-PERSON SCHEME — TO ALL COLLEGES

*a) To women: CSU and Caius MCR have joined to extend the Caius MCR original scheme. Starting Wednesday 14th May, it will now be as follows: if you ring at the times below someone will be sent immediately to your home. If you are worried please ring Cambridge ***** between 9 pm and 10 pm (Caius MCR) and Cambridge ***** (CSU) 10 pm to midnight. Two people will come immediately.*

(CSU is open all day if you wish to ring during normal office hours.)

b) To anybody: if you can spare any time to help out and go to spend a night somewhere to provide protection, then please go to Caius MCR by 9 pm any evening — with sleeping bag if possible.

You will only have to stay for a very short time, to give us your names. When calls come through requesting people for protection, a taxi will be sent to your College or accommodation to pick you up and take you to the specified house. PLEASE help out in this way if you can spare the time.

C. Simple precautions:

1. Keep all windows and doors etc locked.

2. It is a good idea to put locks on the inside of internal doors. This means that even if entry is gained to a kitchen for instance, no further progress into the house can be made.

3. Phone the police special number (*****) if anything suspicious occurs.

*****

That night I was sent out — with Philip, a first-year Caius economist — to 9 Harvey Road, which was filled with unmarried mothers. This was a particularly easy assignment for me, as I lived in a Caius lodging house in the same street at that time. We had been called out by Josephine, who was to become a "regular customer" of the scheme. We chatted till midnight, and then Philip got the spare bed while I slept in an armchair. The next morning, I left around 7.30, but Philip stayed behind — I suspected he had something of a crush on our hostess.

On the evening of the 20th, I went to CSU, and met Philip who was going home as there had been no calls, and Josephine had reported that she did not need anyone that night. I manned the phone for a while, in the company of a strange and very religious

CSU/CAIUS RAPE SECURITY

BODYGUARD SERVICE

CHANGE OF PUBLICISED ARRANGEMENTS

1. IF YOU WOULD LIKE OVERNIGHT BODYGUARDS

ring CAMB **56454** **9 PM to** MIDNIGHT

2. IF YOU CAN HELP OUT AS A BODYGUARD –

Please come to CSU – 3, Round Church Street
at 22·30 on EACH or ANY day – bike & sl. bag if poss

CSU COMBINATION SCHEME AS PREV. PUBLICISED

student whom I will call Tom. Josephine suddenly turned up in person, asking for guards, so Tom drove me and her to Harvey Road. However, Josephine found Tom extremely odd, and told him so, and he drove off in a huff. We therefore sent for a replacement, and Philip arrived! After a game of scrabble it was time for bed — Philip was reluctant to let me have the bed this time, but we tossed for it, and he lost.

On the 22nd I had to discuss Tom with Richard Jopling because increasing numbers of girls were having problems with him. Richard telephoned Tom's vicar to ask him to stop Tom volunteering. That evening I went to CSU and found Richard there — he had already turned Tom away. My veterinary friend Jonathan went out to Josephine's with Philip. I managed to avoid being paired up with Robert, a student from St John's College, who used to take a toolkit with him and mend everything in the house! He had told me he had joined the scheme because he disapproved of extramarital sex! And he also found Josephine "creepy". In the end I returned to 16 Clare Street, where the young mother I had guarded on the 17th now also had an Italian girl and a German-Swiss girl in the house. She informed me that Tom had come to them the evening before and shouted "Rape Protection Service" through the letterbox!

The following evening found me on duty at Josephine's again, while Philip was assigned the top floor of the same house. The next evening we were there again, and were rewarded with a home-cooked Sunday lunch the following day. I also got some trousers repaired. The scheme did have its perks!

The *Cambridge Evening News* had announced on May 19th that police were planning to carry out saliva tests on every man in Cambridge and the surrounding villages who was 5ft 5ins or under, and aged between seventeen and thirty. This, therefore, ensured that they would miss the rapist, simply because all the girls had been mistaken about his age — except for Gail who correctly said he was in his forties. Months of tests at the Home Office forensic science laboratories in Nottingham on samples of the rapist's saliva and a semen sample from the third rape had led to a breakthrough — it was revealed after the trial that the analyses had shown that he had no sperm, and his blood group was one of a small percentage of the population (he was an "O-group secretor with a PGM-2 factor"), about one in 10,000. The young men were asked to present themselves at Parkside station to give a saliva sample, and a massive follow-up operation would find any man who failed to come forward. Employers and landlords were asked to report anyone of that description leaving his job or flat or the city.

Thousands of bottles were ready at Parkside (it was estimated that there could be 10,000 men in Cambridge who met the criteria), and the Nottingham labs had special teams of scientific officers standing by. At that time, the testing of so many men had only been done once before in Britain, during a murder enquiry in Manchester that was successfully conducted by DCS Naan. The very first man tested in Cambridge, on May 20th, was 34-years old and 5 ft 7ins. tall, but he was a suspect because of an anonymous call which he put down to a grudge. The general tests got underway on the 21st, and it was reported that the men were fairly good-humoured. This was understandable because they obviously accepted the need for the procedure, and of course it meant that they could prove their innocence once and for all and thus escape the constant suspicions which had dogged all of them for months — one said that he had been stopped by police about twelve times and "I am absolutely sick to death of it." Another remarked that "It's the small men who are the keenest, after the girls, to catch this maniac."

POLICE SALIVA TEST

TO ALL MEN'S COLLEGES:

The Police would like every man of height 5ft 5ins or under between the ages of 17 and 30 to go to the Police Station at Parkside, Cambridge any time between 9am and 10pm on ANY day (including Sunday).

If you fit into this category PLEASE help the investigation as much as possible by going in.

Published for the Police by the Cambridge Student Union.

ACCOMMODATION OFFERED

To any woman living alone or in pairs who would like to move into accommodation already occupied by others, who have spare rooms for the duration of the term. Own room. Apply CSU 56454/5.

BODYGUARD SERVICE

If you require an overnight Bodyguard - ring 56454 between 9pm and midnight.

If you can help out as a Bodyguard, please come to CSU at 22.30 on each or any evening, with a bike and sleeping bag if possible.

Saliva testing

Some said they just wanted to get it over with. They were asked to spit into a plastic cup, and the saliva was then transferred to a test tube.

This exercise was spoofed in *Private Eye* of May 30th, in an article entitled "That rapist: shock new move by Knacker": "Inspector 'Knacker of the Yard' Knacker, in charge of the hunt for the Cambridge rapist, has stepped up his investigations with a dramatic master plan. Said Knacker: 'Every male in Cambridge between the age of six and ninety will have to come to the Police Station. He will then be asked the key question: "Are you, or are you not, the Cambridge rapist?" By this method we hope to eliminate a substantial number of innocent people. And if nobody answers yes, it may be an indication that the Rapist is no longer in Cambridge, or alternatively, that he is a liar in addition to his other proclivities — in either case our inquiry will narrow the gap.' Inspector Knacker's I.Q. is 71." Funnily enough, that same issue's cover picture, devoted to the impending referendum on membership of the EEC, was of Michael Foot with a speech balloon saying "Moreover we believe that the Cambridge Rapist is none other than President Giscard d'Estaing!"

On May 27th I manned the phones again from 9 till midnight with Dave Carter, one of the creators of the scheme, and we managed to cover the demand, even though volunteers were dwindling in number. There was a very awkward moment when Tom walked in, but we managed to get rid of him.

The next evening I heard from Richard that he needed guards, so I went out with Andrew, a first-year law student from Jesus College, to 145 Chesterton Road where one flat was occupied by Jennie, a pert and pretty blonde barmaid who, alas, was a policeman's girlfriend! We sat discussing the rapist till 1.30 a.m.

Spoof article published in *Private Eye* May 30th 1975

That Rapist

Shock new move by Knacker

Cambridge, Thurs.

Inspector 'Knacker of the Yard' Knacker, in charge of the hunt for the Cambridge rapist, has stepped up his investigations with a dramatic master plan.

Said Knacker: "Every male in Cambridge between the age of 6 and 90 will have to come to the Police Station.

"He will then be asked the key question: 'Are you, or are you not, the Cambridge rapist?' By this method we hope to eliminate a substantial number of innocent people.

"And if nobody answers yes, it may be an indication that the Rapist is no longer in Cambridge, or alternatively, that he is a liar in addition to his other proclivities – in either case our inquiry will narrow the gap."

Inspector Knacker's I.Q. is 71.

She told me that he wore women's shoes, that police had just found a right palm-print from a deformed "baby's" palm, and that she used to serve a weird young loner with just such a hand in the bar. It sounded intriguing.

On May 29th I went to CSU for telephone duty with Richard. It was a rough evening — we needed lots of volunteers, but at first nobody turned up. Fortunately, after we had done a round-up, we had enough. We decided that the time had come to tell Tom to stop volunteering, but he did not turn up that evening. Two evenings later, when I was manning the phones with Dave Carter, Tom did arrive and, to my own amazement, I heard myself telling him that he was not wanted any more. As on the 29th, we had no guards to cover the few calls that came in, so we had to ring all over in desperation before we could meet the modest demand. This was symptomatic of the times — undergraduates were involved in their exams, which were obviously a top priority, while for others the novelty had turned to boredom. For some time already we had been reduced to sending out single guards rather than pairs.

The following day, Richard bought me a drink for getting rid of Tom! When I went out to guard Josephine that evening, I told her about Jennie's story about the deformed hand. She at once remembered a small weirdo who had one, who used to give her the creeps, and who worked for British Rail. I resolved to tell the police about this the next day because, if the hand rumour was true, this must surely be a welcome lead. Consequently, in the morning I telephoned the Rapeline. A somewhat offhand woman answered, and told me that somebody might call on us. Josephine and I waited till noon, but nobody came, so I rang the police and told them I would go to the station at 2 p.m.

I duly went to Parkside and was shown into the Rape Incident Room where a sergeant took my particulars. He appeared very interested in the information about the deformed hand, but when I tried to get him to confirm the palm story, he remained as tight as a clam, so I was none the wiser.

Some bizarre stories arose around this time. First, it was announced in the *Cambridge Evening News* of May 27th that someone had telephoned the *Daily Mirror* offering to identify the rapist for £5000. He asked the paper to run a personal column advertisement carrying the codeword "Jason" if it wanted further details; it did so, but nothing came of it. The following day the press reported that a copy-cat rapist had struck in Oxford — two girl students had been attacked in their bedsits in the Cowley Road area in a month: "Unlike the Cambridge rapist, he doesn't wear a hood; he isn't particularly short — he is about 5 ft 8 in, and sturdy, aged between fourteen and twenty — and he is a Negro. But he does carry a knife." Meanwhile, the police saliva tests were extended to Newmarket, where stable lads and jockeys were to be sampled, although there were no plans to test Lester Piggott (36), Brian Taylor (35), Frankie Durr (48) or Greville Starkey (35) because they were thought to be too old!

On the evening of June 7th, I was manning the phone at CSU, but it was becoming really difficult to find volunteers — many students had already begun to leave town for the summer vacation. In fact that night I had to send out Paul, a friend of mine and ex-Caian, who was visiting me. Fortunately, he was very keen to help. I myself went to guard Josephine. On the way to Harvey Road I struck up a conversation with a very jolly plain-clothes policeman — Cambridge was filled with them, every night, in dark side streets and back gardens. They were easily recognisable from their identical jackets, with the tell-tale bulge underneath caused by the walkie-talkie. He told me that they would far rather catch the rapist red-handed than rely on forensic evidence alone, as a good lawyer could get him acquitted. He was about to have his wish come true.

The next morning, June 8th, Josephine woke me at 9 o'clock with the stunning news that the rapist had been caught!

Chapter 11
The tenth attack and the capture

In the early morning of June 8th, a Sunday, the rapist entered Owlestone Croft, a hostel used by Addenbrooke's Hospital staff and students from Cambridge Technical College. A 27-year-old Canadian, Miss Jane Sproul, had arrived in Cambridge two weeks earlier to take up an office job as a medical clerk at Addenbrooke's. She was in room 41 in Block C, a single-storey annexe of the hostel when, at 2 a.m., there was a knock at the door. Her boyfriend had left her a little earlier, so she assumed he had come back. She was asleep at the time, wearing a red night-dress. She put the light on and got out of bed. Fortunately for her, the door had been fitted with a safety chain because of the reign of terror which had gripped the city. And even more fortunately, she kept it in place when she opened the door.

She was confronted with a hooded figure dressed from head to foot in black. He began to hack at the chain with a knife, and she screamed as she tried desperately to close the door. Her left arm was slashed and her wrist tendon cut, and she later required an operation at Addenbrooke's. She banged on the ceiling of her room with an umbrella. Oddly, her screams were not heard at first by the other ninety men and women in the hostel, or by the police sitting in a car not far away. But two men did hear her — Harry Jeffries, a 26-year-old factory worker, and Ray Holland, a 27-year-old electrician, were fishing for eels in the River Cam about 200 yards away. They had just caught their eighth or ninth of the night.

According to Mr Jeffries, "All of a sudden there were three blood-curdling, terrifying screams. I turned to Ray and said, 'That's the rapist.' Ray grabbed a fishing knife and I had a chunk of iron. We sprinted to the back of the hostel and searched the grounds. All the lights were on inside. We looked through the windows but saw noone about. Then I saw a man wearing a mask and running like the clappers down a corridor. I tried to kick the front door in to get at him, but it didn't open. Then the caretaker came along and opened the door. I said, 'Get out of the way, there is a nutcase in here'. Ray had gone to dial 999. I searched the corridor but the man had gone." He then went into Miss Sproul's room and saw her cut wrist and the blood on the ceiling, walls and door.

Ray Holland added, "People were holding the girl's arm up. She seemed more angry than upset. She was a sensible girl. She had kept her head and screamed her lungs out for someone to hear."

Once the alarm was raised, more than ninety police who were patrolling the bedsitter parts of Cambridge converged on the area. Bicycle tracks were found near Grantchester Meadows, the recreation ground at the rear of the hostel.

Almost a mile away, at 2.15 a.m., 33-year-old Detective Constable Terry Edwards was in Selwyn Road. He was not there by accident — at least 100 police officers had been patrolling all night, every night, for weeks, taking no meal breaks, sitting up trees and on dustbins in various parts of the city. Terry, who had been on the force since the age of twenty and remained a detective till he retired, showed uncanny foresight: he told me recently that officers were allowed to choose where they would spend these nights, and he always picked Selwyn Road, because it was in the heart of the bedsitland where the rapist had struck several times and because it

Detective Constable Terry Edwards

was close to Owlestone Croft, a hostel which he considered to be at high risk of attack.

Around midnight he had shared coffee and sandwiches in a car with his friend (and erstwhile best man) Detective Constable Paddy Proctor; for some reason, both of them had a feeling that something was going to happen that night. As Edwards put it, "We both said we felt that something was on that night. I don't know why. The weather was heavy, nothing was stirring."

Two hours later, DC Proctor was tending to the terrified and bleeding Jane Sproul. DC Terry Edwards, dressed in a combat jersey, jeans and soft shoes, was between a hedge and an alley in Selwyn Road when he saw a bike without lights coming towards him, ridden by a figure dressed in a bright red coat and black court shoes with gold buckles. The police had been told to stop everyone: "I stayed as was our instructions until it came to me. Then I stepped out and shone my torch into the rider's face and said 'stop — police officer — hold it'. The rider made to swerve past me and I grabbed for the shoulders. Then I saw the long blond hair and thought, 'My God, I've clobbered a woman.'

Then in the struggle the wig came off and I saw a face I recognised although at the time I couldn't put a name to it. I knew when the wig came off I had something. But I was surprised by his strength. He fought like hell and I tried to keep him close to me because I knew he had a knife. He struggled free and ran down the road. I grabbed him again and we both crashed over another bicycle and then into a parked car. He rolled half under the car and I grabbed his arm and rammed my foot into his shoulder and then he couldn't move. A man who lived nearby came out and found the knife on him. It was round his neck on a lanyard with the sheath tucked into the top of his trousers. He was wearing leather gloves. He said nothing to me except, 'All right, all right, you're hurting my shoulder' or something like that." In a television interview,

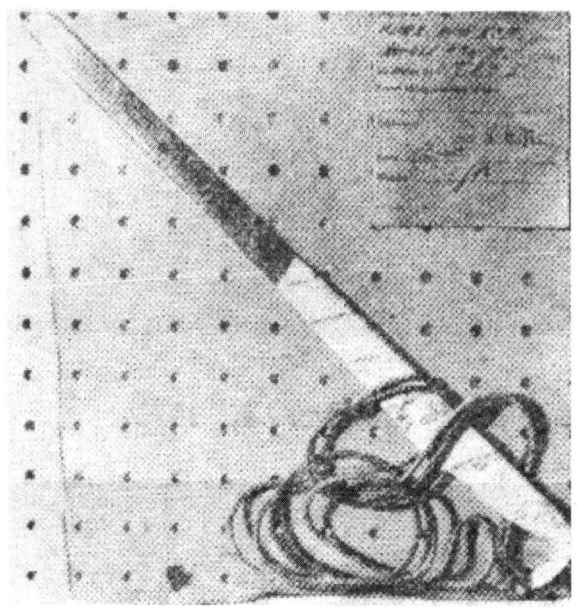

Cook's knife on its cord

Terry Edwards later described fighting the man as "like trying to grab hold of a bar of wet soap!"

As he recently told me, the man was both agile and strong, and above all he did not want to be caught. "When the rider tried to swerve past me", Terry told me, "I grabbed the bike, and he fell off, so the bike was between him and me. He then pushed the bike at me, so I whacked him with my heavy torch" — thus making the mark on the man's face which was still highly visible during his court appearances. "There was a bit of a struggle, but the bike was in the way. He then ran off, but I ended up with him against the wheels of a car. He said, 'Let go, I won't try and get away', but I wasn't falling for that one."

A 29-year-old secretary who lived on Selwyn Road, Mrs Sharon Pearl, reported that she was asleep when she heard a terrific crash "like a bike hitting something." She looked out of the window, and saw a policeman grab a man. Then he shouted to her, "For God's sake, ring the police" (his pocket radio was faulty, so he could only receive with it, not transmit, and so could not call for help himself). She rang them immediately, but it was at least ten minutes before they arrived — reports of two men fighting meant little to a force chasing a rapist at large!

According to Terry, when the police failed to respond to the first call, he again shouted to the woman, "Ring the police, tell them it's DC Edwards and I've got him", along with a few choice expletives — he recalls that the lady later remarked that she had never heard a policeman talk like that before!

The "man who lived nearby" was a decorator, 39-year-old Michael Lawrence, who heard the commotion and went to help the policeman. He said, "I saw a man lying on the ground. Another man was holding his arms. One man shouted that he was a policeman, and I saw he was holding a radio. I grabbed the other man's feet. He was half under a car. I searched him while the other bloke held him down and I found a knife strapped to his chest. There was a struggle, and then police cars arrived."

Subsequently, two black plastic bags were found in Selwyn Road; the rapist had carried them on the handlebars of his blue-and-white woman's bike, which he had stolen two years earlier and used throughout his reign of terror. According to Terry Edwards, "At that time I didn't know anything about what he was carrying on his bike. Later, when he was in the car, I gathered it all up, went back to the station and began labelling it all. I couldn't take it all in at first." The bags' sinister contents were as follows:

- The infamous leather mask with a zipper mouth, a brown beard attached to the bottom at the front, a hair attachment at the back, and "RAPIST" written on the forehead.
- Various blond wigs.
- A black rubber torch, and two spare batteries.
- Pink folded toilet tissues.
- A watch with strap, and a watch without strap.
- An Allenbury's Pastilles tin containing tobacco and cigarette papers.
- A sheath-knife with a brown handle, and a grey-taped sheath on a cord.
- A razor-sharp 9-inch bladed bread knife, with the blade honed narrower than a normal bread knife, to a half-inch depth. It had a white taped handle and a cord lanyard attachment so that there was no risk of him being separated from it.

- An ether pad and ether.

- Four pairs of women's tights.

- Two jemmies.

- A pair of black, imitation leather gloves.

- Several pairs of black and tan coloured tights, knotted into a rope and plaited like pigtails.

- Wire clippers.

- A black plastic hairbrush stolen from the first victim's flat.

- A rubber pipe, eight inches long, with a socket attachment for fusing lights — this device has also wrongly been described as a modified army bayonet. The rapist simply removed a light bulb, inserted the device into the socket and fused the lights.

- A set of skeleton keys (it was thought he had let himself in and out of the hostel with a skeleton key).

- Women's clothes, dresses, women's shoes, more wigs, underwear and make-up.

- Light training shoes with a distinctive sole pattern, imprints of which had been seen at rape scenes.

In short, the bags contained the grisly paraphernalia of the rapist's campaign, and provided all the evidence which the police needed to secure their case. Without it, he might never have been convicted.

After listening to the basic details on the radio that Sunday morning, I left Josephine and went straight to Parkside Police

Station in my capacity as the current organiser of the bodyguard scheme. I needed to know if I could safely shut down the now barely-viable operation.

A beaming DS Hotson pumped me by the hand, and thanked me and my colleagues for what we had done. He could not, of course, tell me anything official, but the ordinary coppers confirmed that they did have the rapist in custody, and that the scheme could be stopped. I asked the police if they had been gentle with him: "Not really, he's in a mess." "Did he 'fall off his bike'?" "Several times!" Jennie told me that she learned from her policeman boyfriend that the rapist had to go to Addenbrooke's hospital before the police station, but in fact this was completely untrue, as has been confirmed to me by both Terry Edwards and Bernard Hotson.

On the Sunday afternoon I was in Caius, doing some work, when Richard popped in for a chat, as pleased as punch, so I was able to tell him what had happened at Parkside. and of DS Hotson's praise and gratitude for Richard's brainchild, the bodyguard scheme. That evening, like the whole population of Cambridge, I was glued to the TV, drinking in every detail of the news.

DC Terry Edwards, meanwhile, was celebrating with DC Proctor that sunny afternoon, drinking champagne on a back lawn. But, as he later insisted modestly, "I am nothing special in this. It could have been any of the boys who got him. I just happened to be in the right place at the right time." As DCS Naan put it, "Edwards took a risk, thank God, by grabbing at what appeared to be a woman on a bike. He could have been ripping off the hair of the wife of the vice-chancellor of the university."

The arrested man was reported to be Peter Samuel Cook, aged 46, a van driver for Dolamore's, a wine firm, married with no children, who lived in a caravan at Villa del Sol, Limes End, Hardwick — a village five miles west of Cambridge. Once he was at Parkside station, his 33-year-old wife Margaret went to visit him, and during the evening DS Hotson drove the couple to their blue-and-green painted caravan home next to a bungalow where Cook's parents lived. They stayed ten minutes, and then Cook was returned to his cell, and his wife wept as he was taken away.

One press report later claimed that Cook had refused to talk for the first few hours after his arrest; but Bernard Hotson has recently informed me that in fact he was not interviewed for several hours for the simple and very sound reason that he could not then plead later that he had been questioned while tied up.

Peter Cook's caravan

The following day, of course, the local and national newspapers had this story plastered all over their front pages. The rapist was already big news nationwide, and his capture even more so. The *Cambridge Evening News*, naturally, had the first photographs of the man himself, hiding his face as he was led into and out of court. He had appeared in the city magistrates' court that morning, and was charged with seven rapes, one attempted rape and one act of grievous bodily harm (on Miss Sproul). According to the paper, "A horde of screaming women mobbed the man...as he was led handcuffed into the court. But police held the women back and the man got into court unscathed." A crowd of about 500 people had gathered outside the Guildhall, and when the car carrying Cook and three detectives pulled up at the rear entrance, a section of the crowd surged towards him, with women shouting jeers and insults such as "Pig!", "Lynch him!" and "Hang him!"

Most of the waiting crowd, however, did not even get a glimpse as he was taken into court through the magistrates' side entrance, whereas most people were at the main doors. Inside, the tiny courtroom was packed with thirty-seven members of the public, a dozen policemen, legal staff and sixteen pressmen. Cook's wife and elderly parents were not present. The hearing lasted no more than three minutes. Cook, wearing a blue/grey suit and a blue open-necked sports shirt, stood with his head bowed, his face grazed and bruised. He was handcuffed between two detectives, while eight police officers encircled the dock. Halfway through reading the charges, the clerk of the court, Mr George Dean, asked, "Do you hear me all right, Mr Cook?", to which he replied, "Yes", without raising his head. After the charges had been read out, Mr Dean asked, "Do you understand?", to which Cook again answered, "Yes." In each of the rape charges, the girls' names were given, which led DS Hotson to ask the chairman of the bench to request that the press should not reveal the names, with the exception of Miss Sproul who had not been sexually assaulted (and

Peter Cook shielding his face from the waiting crowds outside
court. DCS Naan is behind him

Waiting crowds

Chasing crowds

whose name had already been made public in press reports). He did this to save the girls as much embarrassment as possible as well as to avoid distressing their families.

Cook was remanded in custody for eight days and was to reappear in court on June 17th. For his exit, police mounted an impressive decoy operation, with a Black Maria police van and a double column of policemen leading from the court doorway to the road, whereas Cook was again taken through a side door and down a bicycle passage at the back of the Guildhall and straight into a waiting panda car. Consequently, the nation's press and television cameramen were hoaxed along with the crowd. After a while, news filtered out that the prisoner had gone out the back door, so the crowd dispersed. It had been intended to transfer him to Bedford jail, but the authorities there would not accept him, and neither would Norwich prison, so it was finally decided that the only safe place for him where he would be accepted was Leicester maximum security prison.

The next morning, June 10th, all the national papers splashed the story of Cook's court appearance, but the *Daily Mail* stole a march on its rivals by clinching the first interview with his wife at the caravan on the Sunday afternoon, and it appeared under the banner front-page headline:

Accused driver's wife speaks

I STILL LOVE RAPE CHARGE MAN

Underneath was a photo of their wedding on August 3rd 1968 at St Mary's, Comberton (her home village). Both are smiling broadly at the camera. In the interview, Mrs Cook declared: "I'll always love Peter. I shall go and see him soon. He's always been very kind to me, and we've had a lot of fun." She said that she met him when he was a foreman on a building site at Bradwell's Court, Cambridge. Then they lost touch, and she got engaged to someone else. The banns were called and the wedding arranged — but then she went back to Cook. Of her wedding to him, she remarked, "Peter wanted it quiet at the Guildhall in Cambridge, but to me a wedding is a big event in a girl's life. I insisted on a white wedding, and Peter agreed. I have a big family and we didn't ask them all — about twenty in all. We didn't have a honeymoon because of the high cost of the white wedding. It was a beautiful day. And such a lovely setting in the church."

With eyes red-rimmed from crying, she continued, "Before I got engaged to him, he had a bad accident when he was in a crash in his bubble car in Germany." After the wedding they bought the caravan which they parked in the garden of his elderly parents' bungalow in Hardwick. In 1974 the Cooks had spent their summer holiday — before Cook began his raping spree — on the Norfolk Broads in their cabin cruiser, the *Margaret Rose*. At home, according to his wife, Cook liked to watch good films on TV. He rolled his own cigarettes, but neither he nor his wife drank unless they went out for a meal with her sister.

When her husband made his court appearance, Margaret had gone to work as usual — as a bookbinder for Cambridge University Press. As she told the journalist, "I'm over the initial shock. I'll still keep going to work. The people there are kind to me and understand. I can have any time off I wish, but I'd rather be busy. The difficult time is the night time. I cannot drive, and I've arranged for my brother to pick me up in the mornings to take me to Cambridge, but he has to go early — 7 a.m. The police still have our Land Rover, but I shouldn't think I'd bother to drive."

The question of how to get to work seems to have been of major importance to her: Bernard Hotson has informed me that when she first visited Cook at the police station, on the day of his arrest, one of her first comments to him was "Your dad is going to give me a lift to work tomorrow, but I don't know how I'll get there on Tuesday"!

Mrs Cook also told the journalists that her husband had loved his job delivering for the wine merchants, and greatly preferred it to working on buildings as a bricklayer, which he had done in Spain when they lived in Barcelona for a while. "The wine firm was very good to him. The boss let him go early — at half past four — so that he could pick me up from work and I didn't have to wait about." She added that her husband was rather shy, "although he's good company with members of the family we know well. For instance, two Sundays ago we went with some relatives of mine in our cabin cruiser for the day. Peter bought it two years ago. It has four berths, and is 22ft long, and Peter has made lots of improvements since he bought it. We took my brother and his wife to Ely for the day."

The journalist described the caravan as being fitted with colour TV and stereo equipment, and rows and rows of books. Margaret read a lot on all subjects, and she also liked to knit and do needlework. But "just now the caravan is a bit untidy. Since her husband's arrest, Mrs Cook has not felt like doing much."

******

I remember clearly that my first reaction on reading that interview was, "Well, so much for the psychiatrists' assessment of the Rapist — a loner, living with his mother, and unable to have a relationship with a woman." Hopelessly wrong on all counts. I had heard from a different source about Cook's past as a builder, because a technician in the Archaeology Museum had told me that he had worked with him ten years before at Sindall's, a Cambridge construction firm.

On the evening of June 13th, there was a Caius MCR party in the gardens of Harvey Court, which inevitably also became a kind of celebration of the rapist's capture, which had happened only five days earlier. A friend took photographs of me together with Richard Jopling and Dave Carter, the two leading lights of the MCR bodyguard scheme.

The author (centre) with the two creators of the Bodyguard Squad, Richard Jopling (left) and Dave Carter (right)

The following week, on June 17th, because of my long interest in the case as well as my peripheral connection with it, I was determined to see the rapist for myself during his second appearance in court. This was due to take place at the Guildhall again, at 10.30 a.m., so I arrived at 9.30 to be sure of a place in the small room. I was successful, even though crowds eventually gathered outside once again. This time, however, only about 200 people turned up, and once again they were hoodwinked. At 10.30, a prison van was driven up to one of the entrances to the magistrates' court. The crowd immediately gathered there, with women screaming abuse, and photographers furiously taking pictures of the van's blanketed rear window. The van backed right up to the doors, and the crowd closed in — but then, quietly and slowly, it drew away again, and the crowd realised it had been fooled. Cook had been smuggled in through the main doors this time!

His appearance in court was even briefer than the first time — less than two minutes. Wearing the same outfit as before, he was handcuffed to a single prison officer from Leicester jail. DS Hotson requested that he be remanded again until the 26th, and Peter Soar, a Cambridge solicitor acting for Cook, did not contest this application. Once more, the press were requested not to divulge the names of the victims. Cook was led out of the back entrance with a blanket over his head, and into a van with covered windows, while two decoy panda cars stood at the front entrance. Shouting women banged on the van's sides. His wife was allowed to see him at Cambridge police station for an hour before he was returned to Leicester prison.

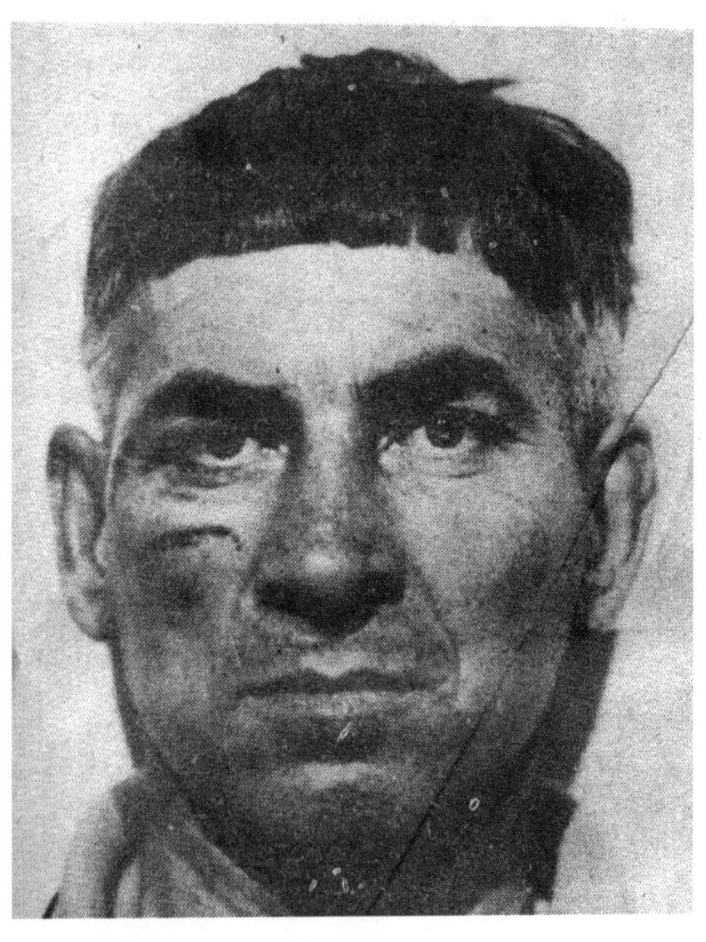

Peter Cook mugshot with bruised and cut face

I remember distinctly my brief view of Cook in the dock. He still looked bruised, and I described him in my diary as an "evil-looking little sod." He was small, but looked quite burly and broad-shouldered. His face seemed strangely familiar but I could not place it. All was revealed later that day when the *Cambridge Evening News* appeared. On its front page was a huge portrait photograph of Cook. Being able to see him properly for the first time, I immediately remembered that I had sometimes seen this unpleasant little man making wine deliveries behind the bar in my college. In fact he had last delivered wine to the Caius bar on the first Wednesday of June, only a few days before he was caught.

But how did the newspaper get hold of this picture? In those days, it was the *CEN*'s custom to approach people in the streets of Cambridge and ask them a particular question, usually about a topical issue. A selection of their answers and opinions would then be printed together, with each quote accompanied by a photo taken of the speaker at the time. This weekly feature was called "What You Think", and someone at the paper had twigged that a certain Peter Cook had appeared in one of these features late in 1974, answering a question about fee-paying education! Cook must have found it highly amusing at the time that a portrait had been published of the very person that the police were desperately searching for, but absolutely nobody was aware of who he was.

On June 26th Cook appeared again at the court, but this time the crowd was smaller (about 150), and no decoy tactics were necessary. He was sent for trial at Norwich Crown Court. One of the charges had been amended — for the attack on Janet D., at Homerton College, the charge was changed from one of rape to one of committing buggery. Once again, a request was made for the press not to reveal the victims' names; and once again, Cook's wife was able to spend some time with him before he was returned to jail.

The three CEN portrait
photographs of Cook

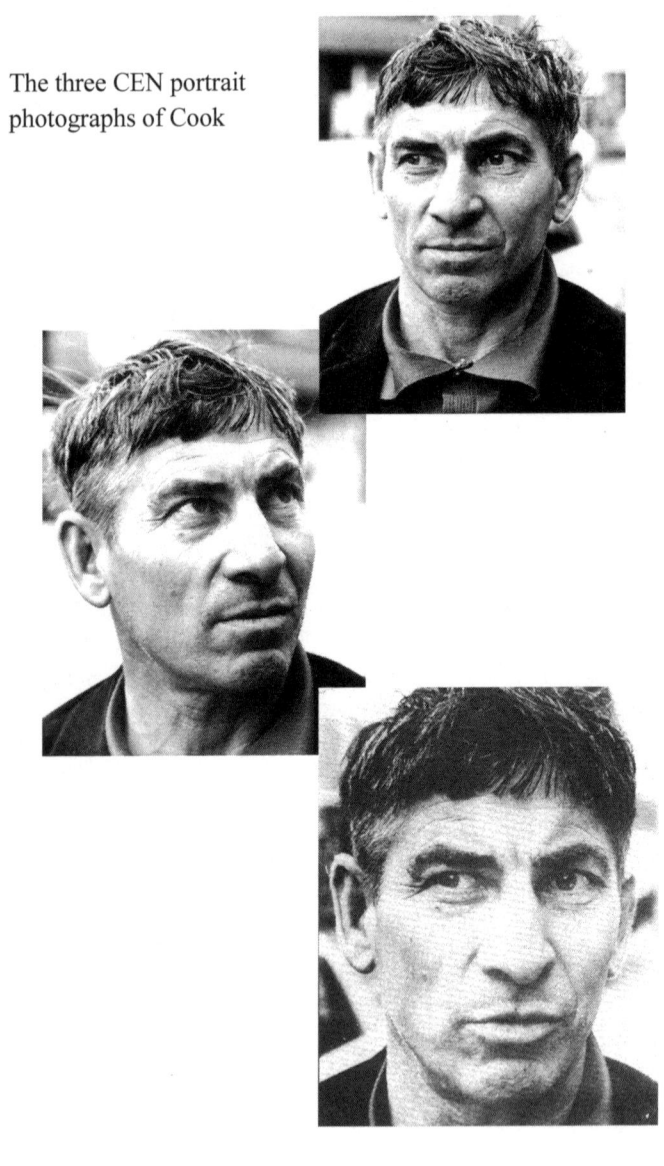

Chapter 12
The Trial

Cook being led out of court by DS Hotson

Cook's trial took place on October 3rd, 1975, at Norwich Crown Court. At seventy-five minutes, it was mercifully brief, since he pleaded guilty to all the rape and wounding charges (but not guilty to two charges of attempted rape and wounding with intent to cause grievous bodily harm), so the victims were not required to undergo the terrible ordeal of testifying. The *Cambridge Evening News*, later that day, carried the front-page headline "COOK GETS LIFE", and no less than six full pages of that issue were devoted to the whole story of Cook and his crimes — largely produced by the in-depth investigations by chief reporter Fulton Gillespie. The national press also ran numerous prominent stories the following day.

DS Hotson told the court what had been learned about Cook's criminal history going back to 1938 when he was only nine. He had done terms of imprisonment until he was sent to Broadmoor in May 1966, where psychiatrists had examined him. He was released in November 1967 because he was found not to be a suitable person for that institution, and he could not be improved. A recent Leicester prison report was also quoted, that "there was nothing wrong in his head," and "he can be dealt with within the confines of the prison system." In answer to a question from the defence, DS Hotson said that throughout Cook's record there were no offences with violence or sex involved.

The case for the prosecution was presented by John Marriage QC and lasted about fifty minutes. The speech for the defence by Brian Higgs QC lasted twenty-three minutes; it told of Cook's revelations about his interest in pornography. In 1972, a few years after his marriage, he bought a pornographic magazine of the kind openly sold in shops, and this led to an addiction to pornographic films. According to Mr Higgs, "These films depicted violence and obscene acts that he could not and would not practise on his wife." Later he was driven to commit the first of the rapes. Quoting from Cook's statement, Mr Higgs said that he felt that it was like a "living hell. The films control me." He claimed to have an uncontrollable urge to do what he had seen on the screen. He claimed that the first rape was unplanned — he had not expected to encounter Frances A. in her home, but when he saw the young girl, scantily clad, he decided to attack her. As he told police, "I came to rob and I stayed to rape," which is precisely what he told the girl at the time.

He had stripped naked after every attack and washed himself completely; he also said in his statement that he had never used the clothes he raped in for anything else. He also claimed that he had no intention to injure anyone, and the knives had been carried to frighten his victims, not to hurt them — a somewhat astonishing claim in view of the last rape, and, especially, the last attack in the hostel.

It was also revealed that, after the first rape, Cook had telephoned a day or two later to see if the girl was all right, and he had asked the landlady who answered the phone where the girl was now living, but she had put the phone down.

When, after his arrest, he was interviewed by DCS Naan, Cook said, "You know it all. The only way out is suicide. What I have done to these girls makes me sick. I am capable of doing anything when I get into those moods." He then appeared to cry for about five minutes, but without a tear, and asked to be allowed to kill himself, banging his head not on the wall but on a blanket. During his interrogations, Cook made constant references to blue films, and later took the police on a tour of the places where he had attacked, and to the hiding places in Hardwick where he kept other gear. He then told DCS Naan, "I must be mad. I'm talking myself into life imprisonment."

The defence also referred to the TV appeal in mid-May by a psychiatrist who was now identified as a Dr Fox. He had asked for the rapist to come forward so that he could be given help. This led to Cook contacting him by phone, when he said that he was suffering from an inner conflict where half of him was trying to do right. Dr Fox had asked Cook to meet him, but Cook did not turn up.

Returning to the question of pornography, Mr Higgs said that Cook's offences were undoubtedly triggered by the films he had been watching — one can therefore see that DCS Naan's early theory about a link to *A Clockwork Orange* may have had some substance to it, even if he had been mistaken about the film responsible. Nevertheless, the judge was unimpressed by the argument, and asked Mr Higgs if he had any evidence to corroborate this theory, and he had not.

Indeed, it is obvious that the vast majority of men who were exposed to the same blue films as Cook did not resort to rape, a point made in the *Guardian* of October 4th by some leading London psychiatrists; and one could reverse the argument and speculate that Cook resorted to pornographic films because he was a potential rapist. On the other hand, Mrs Mary Whitehouse, general secretary of the National Viewers and Listeners Association, predictably seized on the case, stating that it should impress even "the trendy clerics and permissive experts who go into the witness box and defend even the most extreme perversions." She wrote to the Home Secretary, Roy Jenkins, asking for immediate legislation to increase control over pornography.

According to Fulton Gillespie, Cook had been involved in smuggling hard-core porn from the continent, having travelled widely abroad. After his arrest he told doctors that he had been smuggling films and books for the past three years. Sadistic films had completely dominated his thoughts, and his favourite had been one showing Girl Guides being raped. After watching these films, he felt compelled to go out and do the same. He never attempted any form of sadism with his wife, but he sometimes had to take tranquillisers to ease the tension when he felt the urge to go out and do what he had seen.

Ironically, Cook's wife blamed not only pornographic films but also a TV programme. She told the *Daily Mirror* of October 4th that she believed her husband was influenced by the *Kojak* police series — he saw an episode in which a violent rape was carried out by a man armed with a knife and wearing a wig. A few weeks later, Cook became a rapist. "He was fanatical about the *Kojak* shows and never missed one."

However, as the psychiatrists pointed out, few people will act out in life what they have seen in film, and in Cook's case there must have been a disturbance to start with. In other words, this would tend to suggest that there was much in his own character which was to blame. As we shall see below, this was certainly the case. He clearly had a severe personality disorder, and was perhaps a psychopath.

The defence stressed that, while the girls' experiences must have been terrifying, Cook's decision to plead guilty had spared them having to testify, so the judge was asked to give him full credit for that. Another striking aspect of the case, according to the defence, was that Cook's wife was standing by him. During an exchange between the couple while he was in custody, Cook told her, "It was the blue films. I tried to give it up but I couldn't, I'm sorry." Mrs Cook replied, "I told you not to have them. I don't know why you did it." She told journalists that she had sometimes sat alongside him in the caravan, watching blue films such as *Apartment 69* or *Bistro Bordello* on his £150 8mm sound projector but such films did nothing for her. She was prepared to await her husband's release from prison, and the defence considered her "remarkably loyal". During the brief trial, however, she sat in a room beneath the jury box where she could see and hear what was happening but her husband could not see her. She had earlier spent some time with him on his arrival from Leicester prison.

The judge, Mr Justice Melford Stevenson, said, "I would not be doing my duty if I did not impose upon you for each of the counts of rape life imprisonment and it is our opinion that in the context of this case life will mean life." There was also a five-year term for the two unlawful wounding charges, to run concurrently. He then said to the jailers standing at either side of Cook, "Take him away." Throughout the summing up and the sentencing, Cook, wearing a grey suit, pink shirt and blue tie, showed absolutely no emotion. The judge said to him, "You showed no compassion for your victims, you used them to gratify your lust and you terrorised a very considerable community."

Cook's early life

This was not the first time that Cook had unleashed a reign of terror in Cambridge. During the winter of 1951/2 householders had to bar their doors and bolt their windows because Cook had proved himself to be, in Fulton Gillespie's description, an "expert cat-burglar, house-breaker supreme, thief par excellence."

Peter Samuel Cook was a professional criminal. He was born on August 17th 1928 at 60 Cam Road, and spent much of his early childhood at 88 Union Lane, Chesterton, the home of his grandmother. He was always an unruly child — so much so that, by the age of nine, he had burned down his father's shed, and used to tie up playmates and then throw things at them. The family moved to 12 Eastfield, Chesterton, a semi-detached council house, and by 1937 the boy had already come to the notice of police for stealing, and was sent to an approved school, being totally beyond the control of his mother, Dora. A policeman, Sergeant Fred Davison, lived just round the corner from the family, and told the press that he knew Cook well and had to take him to the station many times: "Peter was a natural cop-hater, a lad who always believed he could outwit the police."

His father Sam — whom he seems to have greatly respected — went into the Army and, when war broke out in 1939, Cook tried to follow him to France, but was picked up in Liverpool and taken to another approved school. But as usual, he broke out of there and returned home — this became a constant pattern. In 1943, at the age of fourteen, he went to a nautical training college; then, in May that same year, he took his first job with Marshall's of Cambridge, as a fitter. He left there for Sebro, a firm on Madingley Road, but then, because of persisting thefts, he went to a special training school.

In 1944 he was convicted of housebreaking and sent to borstal. Three years later he was conscripted on National Service to the General Service Corps, then the Royal Artillery, but after only 15 months he was discharged for reasons that are not disclosed on his record. In 1948 he was sent to prison for fifteen months for burglary. He then joined his father's building firm. In 1950 he went to Ireland to work, but by 1951 he was back in Cambridge as a bricklayer and designer — he helped design Bradwell's Court in central Cambridge, a collection of shops which were demolished a few years ago. Nevertheless, crime was his real profession, and he was good at it. It will be recalled that he boasted to Shelley F., "I can break in anywhere", and he was quite correct.

Some astonishing examples of his prowess occurred in the 1950s; at that time, when on the run, Cook used to taunt the police with phone calls and letters — such as a call to DI Breed, saying, "Hello Joe. One of your cars has just gone past. But you won't catch me." Then he would say where he was calling from, but vanish before police arrived. Cook even sent a telegram to the Cambridge CID and informed them that he would be breaking into a house in Hawthorn Way within a few days. The area was staked out by plainclothes policemen. After a few days, with the police still in place, another unsigned telegram arrived, apparently from Cook, which said "Look at number 19." On looking, the police found that the gas meter had been robbed and other property stolen. The occupants had been away on holiday, and Cook had entered the area and the house, and left the house and the area, without the watching policemen seeing or suspecting anything.

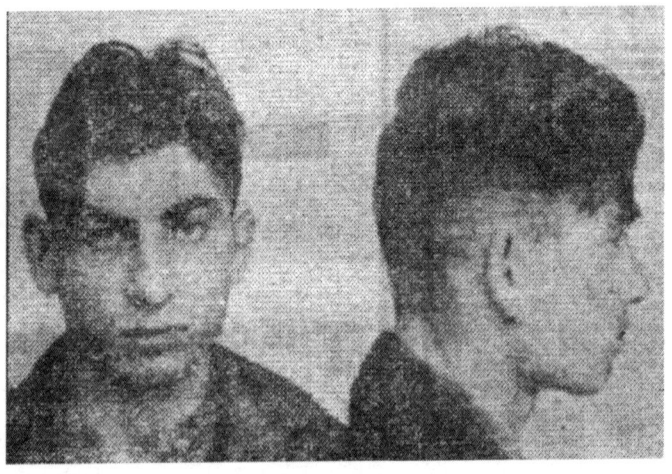

Peter Cook mugshot aged 24

One can readily understand, therefore, that he was never seen going to, or leaving, the scenes of his rapes despite the numerous police patrols. He never made a mistake in that regard. Even on the night of his capture, when he had recklessly attacked a well-lit hostel, he got in without being seen, and even after the alarm was raised he succeeded in getting well clear of the building — his capture took place almost a mile away. Despite the screams, and the fact that the place was swarming with police, he was cool enough to get to his bike on Lammas Land and change into his women's gear on Barton Road.

Cook was equally adept at escaping from places — and not just approved schools! Indeed at one time he was Britain's most-wanted prison escapee. For example, on 28 January 1952, he was sentenced to five years in Dartmoor by Judge Lawson Campbell, who said "Quite evidently you have embarked on a life of crime." Cook was in Shire Hall, awaiting the transport to take him and two accomplices to the prison. He managed to get out, amazingly, through a trapdoor that was 9.5 feet up in the ceiling — according to some press accounts this involved moving a 168lb grille! He stood on the others' shoulders, and then pulled them up after him.

This agility also featured in his work. As a scaffolder he was known as the "Human Fly" because of his ability to tight-rope walk across poles as high as the side of buildings. However, according to Gillespie, another nickname was "The Weasel", because of his sharp and shifty looks (he was also known for his strange sense of humour — for example, when a workmate was up a ladder, he would saw through the lower rungs and leave the man stranded!). After he had broken in somewhere, he would sometimes leave a message in lipstick on mirrors, such as "The Black Diamond has struck", or it might be "The Black Ace", or "The Shadow has struck again" — sometimes he would even leave his initials PSC at the end of these messages, as if to taunt the police. It was an arrogant attitude of "catch me if you can".

On escaping from Shire Hall, he went on the run, and wrote to the *Cambridge Evening News* (which was then known as the *Cambridge Daily News*) that same day about his exploits. As the letter was in red ink, it gave rise to a foolish legend that he wrote it in blood. It was a piece of bravado, boasting to the police that he had been back in Cambridge while they were looking for him, and he had escaped their clutches. In a covering note that accompanied his statement to the newspaper, Cook wrote: "I am not worried now. Police, people, courts, nothing worries me now. I am writing a book, a life story: approved schools to Borstal to prison and maybe prison to the GALLOWS" (His capitals). The newspaper published the letter the next day, January 29th, along with his long statement about his exploits while on the run. However, three months later he was arrested in Glasgow after a chase and brought back to Cambridge, where two years were added to his five-year prison sentence for the escape and for thirty-one offences committed while on the run.

A man who had been an inmate of Dartmoor at the same time as Cook, and who wished to remain anonymous ("I may have to go back one day"), told Gillespie two amusing anecdotes. Once, Cook and another inmate were given the task of doing some repairs in a warden's bathroom in a domestic block. On the first day they spotted a half crown on the window ledge. The other man was keen to take it, but Cook said "No", it was obviously a plant to tempt them so they would lose remission. On the second day it had been moved to the edge of the bath where it was more visible; again the other man wanted it, but Cook made him leave it alone. On the third day, it was on the floor by the door where they could not possibly miss it. This time, Cook borrowed a drill, put a hole through the coin, and then fixed it to a floor joist with a four-inch nail, saying "Now let any b***** move it!"

Peter Cook's letter to *The Cambridge Evening News*

On another occasion, Cook, as a professional bricklayer, was assigned the job of bricking up a wall in the prison. He did so, but fixed a three-foot square area with porridge instead of mortar, but pointed off with cement so it looked perfect. In this way he knew where he could get through if the opportunity presented itself.

During his almost forty years of crime, Cook had been to Barcelona, Ibiza, the Swiss and Austrian Tirol, the Riviera, Belgium and all over Germany, stealing as he went along. In Germany he was deported for stealing from an hotel. In Britain, he had been active in Plymouth, Oxford, Stratford, Stockport, Manchester, Derby and Glasgow. His activities had brought him years in approved schools, Dartmoor, and then Springfield Mental Hospital in London. He escaped from the latter, and fled abroad, but was arrested in Austria in 1960. There he was charged with theft, sentenced to ten months' rigorous imprisonment, and ordered to be deported.

His last major exploit before taking up rape was a series of break-ins in Cambridge in 1965 — at a solicitor's home in Jesus Lane, at the University Pitt Club, and at King & Harper's and Hallens garages. Since he had earlier escaped from Springfield, he was now sentenced to seventeen months in Broadmoor — one reason for this was that he had the ability to roll his eyes upwards until only the whites showed, and he could froth at the mouth at will. He was discharged in 1968, and placed under supervision until early 1970. It was shortly after his discharge that he married Margaret, on 3 August 1968, despite having shown no interest in the opposite sex before then: his father told the *Daily Express* (4 October), "He's never been interested in women and when I have been out with him other blokes might have looked and said that's a nice piece of stuff, but not our Peter... He never had anything to do with girls until he met Margaret and he was absolutely mad on her". His wife told the same paper that "Before we met he never had another girl."

Cook and marriage

Peter Cook's wedding day

(His parents are at left)

	HESP			AND	Spinster of the parish of
bachelor of this Parish					St Wendreda - MARCH - Cambs

WERE PUBLISHED AS FOLLOWS:

1st, on Sunday 18ᵗʰ *February* 1968 by R.Cane

2nd, on Sunday 25ᵗʰ February by R.Cane

3rd, on Sunday 3ʳᵈ March : by

No. 2. **Banns of Marriage** Year 1968

BETWEEN:

Michael John HAWES, bachelor, of the parish of Barton (Cambs) AND Margaret Rose DICKERSON Spinster of this parish

WERE PUBLISHED AS FOLLOWS:

1st, on Sunday 21ˢᵗ January 1968 by R.Cane

2nd, on Sunday 28 Jan by R.Cane

3rd, on Sunday 4ᵗʰ February 1968 by R.Cane

No. 3 **Banns of Marriage** Year 19 68

BETWEEN:

Peter Samuel COOK bach; Parish of St Andrew, Chesterton, Cambridge AND Margaret Rose DICKERSON - Spinster of this parish

WERE PUBLISHED AS FOLLOWS:

1st, on Sunday 2 June 1968 by R.Cane

2nd, on Sunday 9 June 1968 by R.Cane

3rd, on Sunday 16 June 1968 by R.Cane

...and marriage banns

When Cook married Margaret Rose Dickerson, he was thirty-nine, she was twenty-six. The circumstances were rather more fraught than those described in the *Daily Mail* interview with her on June 10th — indeed she later told the *CEN* that "I didn't say any of the things they said. I don't remember half that." The wedding was nearly called off while Cook was in Broadmoor, and Margaret fell in love with another local man and became engaged. The banns had been called, but — according to Margaret — "I suddenly thought of Peter locked away in Broadmoor. I felt sorry for him and went to see him. He promised he would go straight if I married him." When Cook came out, he went to the police saying he was upset about Margaret's engagement and feared for his own actions. He told her that he would come and make a fuss at the church, and he threatened violence, so she called it off. "Afterwards he said he was joking, but I just don't know." The situation blew over, and they got married in Comberton, the village where Margaret had lived all her life — she was described by acquaintances as a "naive village girl". However, she married against her parents' wishes, and her family boycotted the ceremony because they disapproved of her marrying a man who was not only so much older and shorter than she was, but also had a serious criminal record. Her married brothers still lived in Comberton, but her parents had died by 1975.

The couple soon bought the blue-and-cream caravan, and placed it next to his parents' bungalow, Holmdale, which he designed. This was on Limes Road in Hardwick, a village of 500 people. In 1969, Cook joined Dolamore's as a driver, delivering wine to many individuals and institutions — including the canteen at police headquarters! Many people remembered him as always polite and helpful. He earned £27 per week, whereas his wife earned £33 at Cambridge University Press. He took very little part in village life: he could be seen leaving for work at 7.30 a.m. every day, regular as clockwork; he bought his petrol at the village filling station, and had an occasional beer in the local pub, but that was all. He and his wife shopped at the village post office and stores, run by Gordon Coles, who told the *CEN* that they appeared to be a devoted couple, always discussing what they would buy. Other villagers, however, remembered him for some bizarre events. For example, one story was of Cook standing in the moonlight in his night clothes, his hard face contorted with rage as he tried to take on five or six men in an attempt to break up a party near his home, simply because music was still playing at 11 p.m. Another story was of him squaring up to the Cambridgeshire Hunt, ready to be trampled into the ground rather than allow the hounds near his home because he was afraid they might savage his pet cat.

His parents, Sam and Dora, had bought just under five acres of land in Hardwick for £4000 in 1966, and six years later they sold it to Fairview Estates for more than £78,000, thus setting a price tag for the other villagers and bringing prosperity to the place. By the time this "gold rush" ended, eighty acres of Limes Road were in the hands of property firms, and fifty-five villagers had made a total of more than £1 million.

It seemed that Cook's wife would have no financial worries during her fruitless wait for her husband's release from his life sentence — he still had several thousand pounds to his name (£5000 in securities and £3000 in a building society), and their assets also included a Land Rover and a first-class cabin cruiser, as will be seen below.

Cook's sexuality

Although Cook was short, he was small, powerful and agile. However, he was born with a rare genetic disorder, a chromosomal defect which gave him some female characteristics. This was Klinefelter's Syndrome, the symptoms of which are small testes, a small phallus, absence or near-absence of sperm resulting in infertility, and usually gynaecomastia, enlarged male breasts resembling the female. Being short in stature is also a common feature.

In the *Cambridge Evening News* of October 3rd 1975, two women, Mrs Jenny Cartwright and Mrs Connie Jackson, revealed that Cook once told them he had nearly been a woman. They both worked in the kitchen of the "*Bird in Hand*" pub which he frequented almost every day. According to Mrs Cartwright, "It would be the back end of last year when he came into the kitchen and, after some chat, just announced, 'I was nearly a woman once.' I remember saying something like, 'Oh go on,' and he said, 'OK,

I'll show you.' I didn't know what to expect. Then he pulled up his shirt and pointed to two well-marked operation scars on his chest where he said he had female breasts removed. We were dumbfounded. He said he had been embarrassed to go swimming, or that he was fed up with people taking the mickey because he had big breasts. Certainly the scars were exactly where you would expect to find breast operation marks."

Mrs Jackson explained that "He used to come into the kitchen because he didn't like to be with the people at the bar. He would sit and have his meal on his own — ham, egg and chips, or maybe meat pie and always coffee. He never drank any alcohol that I saw. Sometimes he would take away rolls if he said he was busy. Then this day he came in and I don't remember what started the conversation. Then before I realised it, he had lifted his shirt to show us the scars where he said he had them removed. His actual words — I remember because it was such a shock — were: 'I was nearly a woman once.'"

According to Fulton Gillespie, in 1960 Cook went to Pollock Ward in Addenbrooke's Hospital to have his female breasts removed. At the same time a biopsy of his testicles revealed that he had no sperm and could never father children. His testicles and penis were smaller than average, thus confirming, along with breasts, the diagnosis of Klinefelter's Syndrome. He also underwent special chromosome tests, known as buccal smear tests. A woman who was a nurse at that time said that he frightened her, and she was still scared of him in 1975, so she told the *CEN* she wished to remain anonymous: "I remember him among all the patients only because he disturbed and frightened me so much. He would make remarks with strong sexual overtones and stare at you from the corners of his eyes. He was in hospital to have tests done....to determine his chromosomal make-up. I read about the saliva tests in the papers, and I told police that Cook had a similar test in 1960. He also frightened a friend of mine, another nurse, by jumping from the bushes at the nurses' home in Owlestone Croft and throwing pornographic pictures in front of her." But he is not known to have ever assaulted anyone, sexually or otherwise, before 1974. It is ironic that it was that same hostel of Owlestone Croft which was to be his downfall.

It is important to note that his five-year sentence to Dartmoor was for store-breaking, and what he had stolen from Boyton and Wright's, a shop in High street, Chesterton, was women's clothing: six women's pyjama sets, eight underslips, two jumpers, six cardigans, four twin sets, four silk undersets, four headscarves, fifty-five bottles of perfume, nine boxes of powder and four lipsticks (it is also rumoured that he was discharged from the army for dressing up as a woman). Twenty-three years later, when he was caught in Selwyn Road, he was carrying women's jumpers, tights, lipstick and wigs. He had used the lipstick to leave messages at houses containing prospective victims; as mentioned earlier, phrases such as "Sleep tight — the Rapist" were found on the windows of sleeping girls.

As I had myself suspected, Cook was well aware that police were actively seeking a small man, but not a woman — so he began to dress as a woman when he cycled the five miles in from his caravan at Hardwick. He would then change into his rapist gear near the victim's house, and then change back into his female outfit, complete with wig, and cycle home through the police traps. However, even when dressed as a woman he took no chances. As a criminal with almost forty years experience, he could spot a plainclothes policeman a mile away. If he saw one, or was suspicious of a person or car in the distance, he would dive off his bike into the nearest cover.

It will be recalled from the victims' testimony that, during the attacks, the sex act was quite perfunctory; the rapist effected penetration but little else. However, most of the rapes were preceded by a long and abusive diatribe about what he intended to do and how he hated women. Psychologists can doubtless theorise at great length about the possible links between his chromosomal abnormality and this hatred of women — but not all women, since he seems to have loved his wife.

Cook's family and friends

Sam and Dora Cook, Peter's father and mother

For more than fifty years Cook's father Sam, aged 71 in 1975, had been a well respected city tradesman in Cambridge; he was an expert builder and plasterer, and ran his own business. By the time he retired he left a top-class name for fairness and straightforward honesty, and none of the city businesses with which he had traded for so long had a bad word to say about him. According to the *CEN*, his fellow builders in competition and those who supplied him all spoke very highly of this little bespectacled man who would even help a rival. One said, "Sam Cook was one of the nicest and most genuine tradesmen you could hope to meet. It's a damned shame things should turn out for him this way."

Things had indeed turned out very badly for him where his son Peter was concerned. As mentioned above, he had already gone off the rails by the age of nine, and after that he gave his father and Dora, his mother, nothing but trouble. By the time he got married, his parents hoped things would be different. When Sam sold his land at Hardwick for £78,000, he gave £12,500 to Peter as a help to his marriage, secretly hoping that it would keep his criminal son out of trouble for good. Until the revelation of the rapist's identity, he thought his son had turned over a new leaf, with a steady job and a devoted wife.

Peter Cook spent £2000 on a Land Rover and paid cash — £4000 or £4500 — for a glass-fibre motor boat. To earn extra money, he would tow boats around the country using the Land Rover. At Upware, on Norman Cole's Marina, he kept his superb cabin cruiser. It could sleep four, and was powered by an electric-start 50 h.p. motor. Christened the *Margaret Rose*, after his wife, it was fitted with all navigational aids and sea-going equipment, including a deep-sea echo sounder, a Seafarer Mark III, which was designed for distance sailing on the high seas. Police believed that he may have planned to use the boat to escape overseas if things got too hot — he had escaped to the continent several times during his criminal career. As Mr Cole told the *CEN*,

Peter Cook on the *Margaret Rose*

"It's not the kind of thing one buys for cruising up the Cam. This is an ocean-going rig. It's probably the best boat I've had in the marina. His only subjects were boats and motors. He was a real decent sort. His boat was his pride and joy, and he was an experienced boatman." Boating was Cook's social life, and he used to take the craft up river towards Ely, with his wife, and occasionally friends, on board. Police combed it for evidence, but found nothing incriminating.

Sam told Fulton Gillespie that his son was a man of contrasting styles and moods. He wept as he said, "What can I say to these poor young girls? What can I do? What can anyone do? All I can say is that if I had known, had any idea he was doing this [the rapes], I would have shot him. Maybe it is a hard thing for a father to say about his son, but I really would have done it."

As he spoke outside his neat bungalow, only a week after his son's arrest, he was accompanied by Margaret. Both were still stunned that the man they knew so well was the "beast of bedsitland". Sam continued, "The police came that morning he was caught, and that was the first I had heard about it. It was a beautiful morning. The sun was shining and I had been out with my animals at the back. Then I got the news from the policemen. They just arrived and told me. I couldn't take it in. I was up there one minute, down and smashed to bits the next. I was shattered. I am now a broken man. I am empty. Finished. Nothing left at all. What can I say?" He told another journalist that he never wanted to see his son again: "I have always said he should get life. I would rather he had committed a murder than what he did to those girls. This has killed me inside."

According to the *Daily Express*, he also said, "His mother called him Taf. She used to get very worried, but I can honestly say with my hand on the Bible that I never realised or thought he was the man. If I had done so I would have turned him in, even though he was my only son. He has broken his mother's and my heart. He was her pride and joy and she doted on him... It is not long ago that his mother gave him £1000 because he had been specially kind to her, and soon after she gave him more money in pound notes because she was worried about the future. I will never go and see him again. When he has been in prison in the past I went to see him but that was crime and different. I feel more sorry for the victims than him. I would kill him for what he has done if I got the chance. I know he's my only son, but he has done wrong, a lot of wrong, and he's got to be put away for a long time. I disown him completely."

Referring again to Dora, aged 73, he told the *CEN*, "My poor old girl is in there, really ill. It has nearly killed her. The doctor has given her pills, but she is suffering. I never leave her alone. A neighbour is with her now." She herself later told the *Daily Express*, "I am terribly distressed. My heart is broken. He's my only boy. I don't know what to say. I cannot believe it." She had started to spy on Cook when he kept on going out late at night, creeping out of the bungalow and going to his caravan, but she never managed to catch him — in any case, the worst she suspected was that he had gone back to burglary.

The *CEN* also asked Margaret, Cook's bespectacled plump wife, if she had suspected anything during the eight months of her husband's terror campaign: "No, not a thing. I had no inkling. I just couldn't believe it." In the *Daily Express* of October 4th, which described her as quietly-spoken and rosy-cheeked, she was quoted at length as follows: "Of course I still love him. I have forgiven him. He's my husband. I have told him since his arrest that I still love him and always will. He knows I am the only woman for him, and he is the only man for me. I'll stand by him till the end of my days. I'll wait for him. I know people may think I knew what was going on, but I honestly did not. If I had known I would have stopped him. I did so once before many years ago, after he broke into a house, and I would do it again. I don't know why he did it. We were happy in every way.

He says it was all due to blue films. He got them from a shop in Cambridge, I think. He showed me one but it bored me, and I was disgusted and not interested. He did not go out much at night. When he got these films he used to say he was going out to a show with a gang of fellows. He was always back about 2.30 a.m., and I had no suspicions at all. When we saw about the rapes on television we used to laugh and joke, and once I said, 'It cannot be you, it looks nothing like you.' I also said that if it was him I would tell the police, but he said it was not him and I never dreamt otherwise. He said police would never get the man because he was too clever for them. He told me the police had questioned him a couple of times, but he said it was not him and I believed him. There was no reason why I shouldn't."

She repeated that she naively believed him when he accounted for his nocturnal absences from home by saying he had been at late-night sex film shows. He always managed to get back to Hardwick before she woke in the mornings; and on the Sunday morning when he was arrested and did not return home, she thought he had got up early and gone to his workshop at the back.

"Perhaps [the films] gave him the same kicks as he used to get out of being a burglar but that was all behind him. I have always been the only girl for him, and that goes back to the time when I first left school and got a job. We went on the Continent together while he was on the run in 1965 — he had a crash on the autobahn and has a steel plate in his head."

We have been very happy in every way. I knew all about his past but he promised me he would go straight and he has done so until now. That was the condition under which we married. Everything was marvellous for us... we had just got planning permission for a bungalow down the lane... I have thought of suicide since this. I feel sorry for the girls. I'll wait for him whatever happens. He says he still loves me. He's my husband and the only man for me." Touching words but, since Margaret Cook denied much of what was reported in the earlier *Daily Mail* article, one inevitably wonders how much of the *Express* interview was accurate.

The same newspaper also featured another startling and unique piece of testimony that day: an interview with David Thompson, said to be Cook's closest friend, illustrated with a photo of Thompson driving Cook's boat, with Mrs Cook smiling broadly next to him. Thompson, 33, was a self-confessed triple killer who had spent the last eleven years in Broadmoor. He had been out on licence since January and was now living in a London hostel and working at a London factory. The friendship between the rapist and the man who admitted shooting his young wife and her parents at their home in Plymouth twelve years before began in 1965 when Cook was admitted to Broadmoor. "Cook was a burglar at the time, but in order to escape a long prison sentence — according to Thompson — he feigned madness.

When the police visited me after [Cook's] arrest, they put the fear of God into me. I just could not believe it at first. Then suddenly I thought, 'Did the police think I knew about the attacks?' Here I was trying to start a new life on the outside, only to find that I had become friendly with a sex maniac. I told them all I could about Peter. I told them of visits I had made to his home at Cambridge. All about his boat and of his blue film shows. Peter had many films and I was one of the people who gave him one. I did not know they gave him the urge to attack women.

During one of my trips to Cambridge , when the attacks were all the talk, Peter discussed them with me. Now when I look back on the conversation I realise he was trying to tell me something. He would talk about the rapist in the third person, saying things like,

'You know, this guy is obviously a candidate for Broadmoor. He will end up there with the other nutters. He is doing this out of compulsion. If he is not stopped, he is going to kill someone. Someone must stop him before he goes too far.' I realise now that he was talking about himself.

I have seen many dangerous men in my time there. But Peter Cook never struck me as being a vicious man. He was a loner like me. He was quite intelligent, and seemed a cut above the average Broadmoor inmate. I would not have kept up my friendship if I had known him to be a violent sex man. All right, you might say, who am I to talk — I killed my lovely wife and two other people. But it was all done in one mad set of circumstances. God knows, I have paid for it by being locked behind those doors for eleven years with raving lunatics... the assaults on those women shocked me. Those kinds of attacks are despised even by Broadmoor men. I believed Peter when he told me that he was a burglar who had 'worked his ticket' into Broadmoor rather than do time in prison. When he was released he and his wife visited me regularly and told me that I would always be welcome at their home. When you have been in Broadmoor there are not many people who will welcome you."

Sam likewise told of Peter's kindness, but also his callous cruelty. He recalled a son with a volatile and complex personality who would do anything for people he liked, and who would raise his cap to neighbours in Hardwick. There was one remarkable story involving Detective Inspector Joe Breed, who was chief of Cambridge CID in the 1950s, and who had locked Cook up several times in that period. Cook wrote to Breed and his wife Mollie threatening to kill them — yet years later ended up being their friend until Breed's death in 1975.

Mrs Breed told the *CEN*, "I shall always remember the day Peter Cook said he would kill me. I didn't know him then, that was when we lived in Greville Road. I can even remember what the letter said. I haven't kept it, but I shall always remember it in its blue envelope. I know Peter thought a lot of Joe although he caused Joe a lot of trouble and Joe put him in prison for a long time. He also wrote to Joe and threatened to kill him, but we were never worried, although the neighbours were terrified. I never knew a lot about Joe's work, and I never asked him, but Joe always hoped until his last days that Peter would go straight. There seemed to be some bond between them, Joe and Peter, as there was between Joe and most of his customers.

Peter came to the house here when Joe was taken ill, and he always acted as a real gentleman. He brought Joe a bottle of sherry, and he even produced the receipt to show Joe he had bought it. He also called with flowers when Joe was in hospital. You could never believe it was the same man who was doing the rapes at the time he called at the house. One day he told me he wanted to adopt a child, but they would only let him have a handicapped child. Peter said to me, 'What good is a handicapped child to me? What chance would it stand on my boat?'

Once when we went to see Joe in Chesterton — it was one of Joe's lucid moments although he couldn't do much — Peter helped him with his bingo card. Then he mentioned he had been pulled in by the police who were looking for the rapist. Peter said, 'I told them I was not going to talk to anyone what hadn't got any stripes on his arm,' and we had a laugh about it because Peter was always cheeky when he got caught, and he was very good at getting away. Joe said to him then, 'But you wouldn't do that, would you, Peter?' Now I think of it, he turned his head away and he didn't answer. That didn't occur to me until I heard the news on the radio on Sunday evening. You know, it's just unbelievable. When he was here at the house Peter was such a gentleman — a real gentleman. I'm glad Joe is not here to see or hear about all this. It would have broken his heart."

One strange testimony to the relationship between Breed and Cook emerges from a reminiscence by Bernard Hotson. When he first visited the infamous caravan on the evening of the day of Cook's arrest, he spotted a copy of *Moriarty's Police Law*, the police bible, and on its flyleaf was an inscription to Cook from Joe Breed! Hotson also recalled that he had met Cook for about five minutes in the 1960s, just after taking over in Cambridge from Joe Breed as DCI. Cook came to see him, introduced himself as having known Breed, and told Hotson that he was planning to set up a burglar alarm business!

Another striking aspect of Cook's personality was that he loved animals, and for years in the 1960s kept monkeys in a shed in the garden of his family's home in Chesterton. He would amuse friends by imitating their antics. Oddly, when he fell foul of the police in his pre-rape days, he would often dance around his cell jabbering like a monkey, and then sit for hours, curled up in a corner, with his hands on his head like a monkey. His simian habits extended into his crimes in those days, because he would leave sugar, cooking oil and sauce splashed on the walls and furniture of the places he broke into, and he would urinate into wine glasses, cash boxes and tills. He would also sometimes leave messages, some of them obscene, on walls or mirrors, and he would slash cushion covers and stuff them full of flour.

Police always knew when he had done a job because of the mess he left behind.

Tellingly, on the day of his arrest for the rapes, his one request was, "Can I go home and see my pet cat?" After police had driven him around Cambridge, so he could point out the places he had attacked over eight months, they granted his request and took him home in handcuffs. He was led up the shingle path to his caravan, but the cat had gone hunting!

Cook with monkey

Cook's caches and stashes

Cook was supremely cunning at concealing things from both family and the law. For example, he would often supply friends with blue films, and police recovered some reels from those he supplied, but mostly they recovered them from the hiding places in nooks and crannies that were strewn over 2.5 acres behind his caravan in Hardwick. The caravan — which was called Villa del Sol after his favourite Spanish hideout, where he would go in the late 1950s and early 1960s when he was wanted by the police — was always "clean" when searched. Cook was far too clever and experienced to keep anything incriminating on open view.

Already in the above-mentioned statement that he sent to the *Daily News* in 1952, Cook had boasted of his hiding places. He had heard that D.I. Joe Breed had been searching his father's garden shed for stolen jewellery. He wrote: "You don't suppose I would hide jewels in my own shed under a slab floor. I have better hiding places. That's the reason I came back, for the loot and cash also passport. I have hiding places by the river. In fact I have stuff in the river. It's safe. The river was just one place, but it was a little late to go diamond diving on Monday the 14th [of January 1952]."

This helps explain why it was no less than three weeks after his arrest in 1975 that police finally discovered Cook's elaborate hiding places and their amazing contents. Detectives found 600 items under the floorboards of an old shack behind his caravan. There was a secret sliding-door compartment under and behind a saw-bench, camouflaged with boards. The items were all neatly stored in plastic bags and airtight cigarette boxes. They comprised:

- An up-to-date passport in his name, taken out for a 10-year period in 1970, together with 1800 pesetas carefully folded inside.
- Changes of clothes, both male and female.

- 22 wigs, some of them short-haired, others long; hair-pieces, pig-tails and pony-tails tied with ribbon. These had apparently been stolen from bedsitland over the previous two years.

- The dark glasses and blonde wig which were accurately described by the witness who saw Cook on his bicycle in Pye Terrace on May 6th.

- A bottle of ether and rags.

- A variety of stolen women's clothes and underwear — bras, panties, suspender belts, etc.

- Women's shoes and knee-length boots.

- Piles of lipsticks, eye shadow and make-up.

- Handbags, make-up bags and toiletries.

- Jewellery and trinkets, including women's wrist watches, bangles, brooches, beads, necklaces and ear-rings.

- Various sexual aids, apparatus and contraceptives, and false breasts.

- Three large red exercise books packed with clippings from the *Cambridge Evening News* about the rapes.

Wig with glasses

Torch on a rope

Bottle of ether

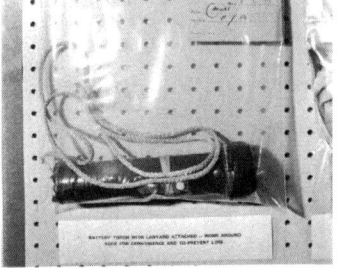

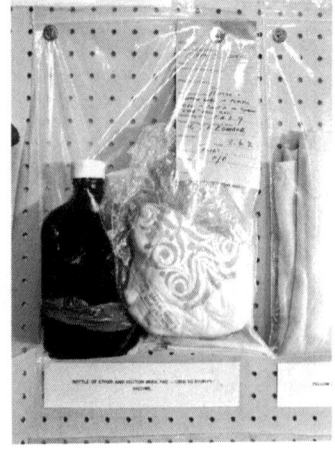

Part of Cook's knicker collection

By far the most sinister items, however, were:

- A red hardback notebook, cut into three parts (2 x 4 inch mini-directories), that listed days, dates, flats, girls, keys, phone numbers, addresses and plans of the internal layout of flats.

- Dozens of airtight tins and zip-up vanity bags jammed full of hundreds of keys to girls' flats and college hostels, and skeleton keys. They were carefully labelled — each had a tab attached with the relevant address.

Over many years, Cook had entered hostels and flats and stolen keys lying around, as well as items of women's clothing, and newly arrived letters. The addresses on the tabs revealed that there was hardly a street in all of Cambridge's bedsitland which he had not visited — and for each address, a key had been stolen or made to fit the chosen victim's door. To give just one example of his research and knowledge, when police confronted him with bunches of keys, he simply looked at them and said, "Oh, those relate to New Hall." He could also recognise keys from many other places.

The notebook was simply chilling. It contained a macabre directory of potential victims, meticulously compiled. Each key was listed in it. The entries were made in separate columns, coded and numbered. All of the houses he had attacked up to the time of his arrest were listed. According to the police, the system was as follows: the first column gave the date when he first checked the house; the second had the code F/H; the third gave a shortened form of the address; the fourth was left blank or carried the code

Peter Cook's notebooks

K; the fifth had the code F/G followed by numbers; the sixth contained the phone number; and the last had personal details of the girls, and sometimes ink sketches of the flat's internal layout. So, for example, an entry such as "13/4 F/H 57 Marsh K G 3-4" translated as "Checked on April 13; Flat-cum-house at 57 Marshall Road. I have a key. Three or four girls live there." Having noted the phone number from the accommodation ad in the paper, he would ring the number in the daytime. If there was no reply, he knew the coast was clear to break in and check out the flat.

After his arrest, Cook told police that he even knew which back garden backed onto which house, where there were fences with loose panels for access to and from lanes and alleys, and which roads the alleys were linked to. This tremendous knowledge of Cambridge shows why he was so hard to catch — he could move across the city without using a single main thoroughfare!

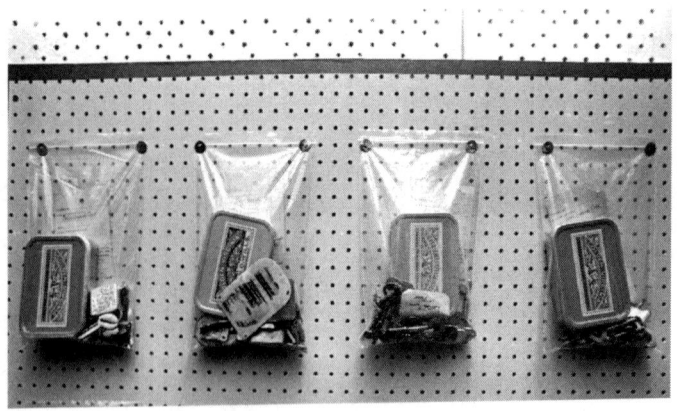

Part of Cook's key collection in tobacco tins

Police believe that he had used many of the keys to enter houses, not only to steal but also to establish if they were occupied by girls. He would check wardrobes for men's clothes, and would then mark the key either H/F or F/G — H meant house, F was flat, the second F was female, and G was girl. If he was unable to assess the tenant's age from her clothes, he would simply use "F" for female, but if the clothes indicated a young woman, he would use "G".

But his research was even more meticulous and detailed than that. He would establish the name from accommodation advertisements in the *Cambridge Evening News*, from electoral rolls in the public library (he told police after his arrest that he spent hours combing the rolls there), or from letters and newspapers delivered to the house. He would then enter the name in his red notebook. He sometimes kept the letters, and police found some under the floorboards.

He singled out groups of girls for careful, special observation. He did this in the daytime when he was delivering wine. If a house had a back garden, a nearby alley or its surroundings provided good cover, this was all noted down on his list. Armed with all these details, he would then start watching the girls' movements. Such was his skill and accuracy in "casing" the houses that he was always able to attack when a girl was on her own. Moreover, such was his skill as a housebreaker that any flats difficult to assess from the outside were broken into first so that he could check the layout.

For example, in the houses attacked on Huntingdon Road and Pye Terrace the inner layout of the flats was hard to imagine from outside: Huntingdon Road was small and compact, with internal steps up, and awkward corners; while Pye Terrace was also small, with a step down into the kitchen, an awkward step up at the top of the stairs, and a step down into the back bedroom. So Cook broke into both places ahead of his attacks, and made mental notes of the one-step-up places. He later drew the layouts in his notebook. This meant that if he returned in the dark, he would know exactly where the potential stumbling places were located if he needed to make a swift exit.

Another aspect of his cunning was the use of disguise. The presence of both short- and long-haired wigs is explained by the fact that, on his first raping expeditions, he wore two wigs. The shorter one was fixed to his head with hairpins and glue, while the longer one was put over it loosely. This is why Elizabeth C, in his first, failed attack on Huntingdon Road, after managing to tug off his top wig, was fooled by the other wig into thinking that he was a younger man with a modern hairstyle. Later, however, the wigs became superfluous during the attacks once he adopted the leather hood.

Cook had made his infamous hood himself. The national press, on the other hand, had not unreasonably assumed that it was a well-made and nicely-fitting mask which had been bought from a shop. The *Times* of May 10th had pointed out that such leather hoods could not be bought in Cambridge, but cost £12. 75 in Soho. The *Sunday Mirror* of May 11th actually bought two such hoods from different Soho shops, and questioned the shopkeepers about their clients ("Kinky trail of the rapist in a leather hood"). Nobody guessed the bizarre truth — that Cook had made the hood from an old leather shopping bag. He had stuck hair around the bottom to give the impression that he was bearded with long hair. He had made the mouth not from any old zip, but from a heavy industrial-strength one, with long saw-like teeth that fitted into each other like those of an Alsatian. When open, the mouth looked like shark teeth, when closed it resembled what Fulton Gillespie described as "the snarling grimace of a Hallowe'en monster". He outlined the eye holes with white paint, below the word "RAPIST" on the forehead. Cook told police that he put the hood on because it saved him having to introduce himself [*sic*], it enabled him to carry out rapes with the light on, and it terrified the girls so that they did not attempt to fight him off.

Despite the media's red herring of the Soho shops, Cook was well known to Cambridge's only sex shop of the time, the "*Love Inn*" on Mill Road, owned by husband and wife John and Pat Morley. John Morley, then aged 35, told the press that, weeks before his arrest, Cook not only bought sex films there but also boasted in front of customers that he was the rapist: "He bought a couple of sex films here at £8 a time, but nothing else. About the last time he came in here he was shouting his mouth off as usual and he said in front of about four or five customers, 'the police keep coming to my caravan looking for blue films and I'm the fucking rapist they are looking for!' We all laughed at him and didn't take any notice. I thought he was a nutter, I am kicking myself now. He was the most foul mouthed, uncouth character I have ever met. He used to come in and ask for blue films. We of course don't sell blue films, we are not allowed to by law. It was impossible to shut the man up, he would talk on and on, shouting at the top of his voice, saying what he liked to do to girls, It was disgusting. I tried to get rid of him but he kept coming in. If I wouldn't talk to him he talked to the customers and we lost a few because of him.

He used to boast that the police were always stopping him in his van and looking for pornographic films, and also going to his caravan. He even boasted that he had been to Broadmoor. He always looked scruffy and wore a dirty old trilby. He carried a bag with blue films in it. I told him I didn't want anything to do with them. All he bought here were Harrison Marks sex films....he was a connoisseur of those and he paid cash." Morley believed that Cook's frequent visits to the shop were part of his cunning plan to avoid detection. "He was a shrewd chap. He does these rapes and then comes to us soon after we open. He knew damn well the CID would come to us as the only sex shop in the city. He wasn't interested in the shop — it was all kids' stuff to him; he had the real

McCoy. He comes in, telling everyone he is the bloody rapist, not just me, the customers as well." Morley had been asked by police to tell them of anyone using his shop who could be the rapist. "I told them about two or three funny looking customers and about one bloke who wanted to buy a mask but I didn't tell them about this Cook bloke because I would not have thought it was him in a thousand years." His wife Pat, 32, added, "I was amazed when I heard it was him. I always called him the weasel. He used to come in about twice a week. He was always going on about his prison record and saying 'I'm always getting blamed for things.'"

Cook was annoyed because after one visit to his caravan, the police had left with many of his pornographic magazines and other material, and he threatened to consult a solicitor to get them back. After his arrest, his van was found by police to contain a large amount of hard-core pornography, including blue films. According to Mr Stan Tyrrell, owner of a boatyard which Cook often visited, "He always talked about sex. He was a nuisance when he came here because he would always start showing the lads his latest hard-porn magazine." Another employee at the yard said, "He carried the porn in his firm's van. It included magazines and blue films and we know he used to show them all over the place but we never got invited."

Case evidence

DS Hotson and DCS Naan stand with Cook's bike in front of the
evidence board

The display of evidence

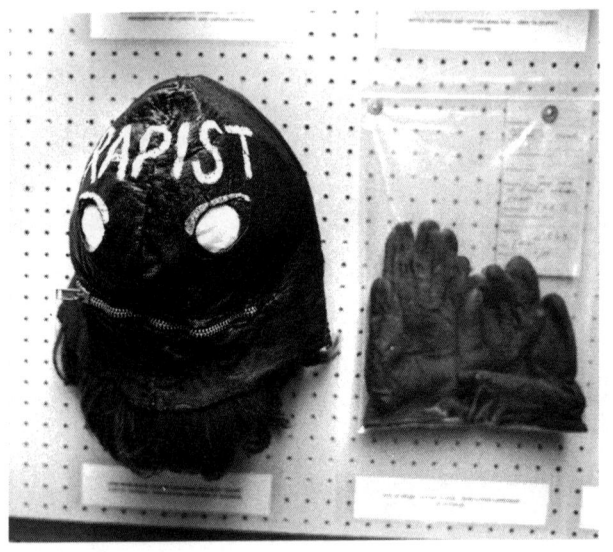

Mask and gloves

Cook: a cold, callous, cunning, clever criminal

Throughout his eight month reign of terror, Cook had gone about his normal work, frequenting students and staff in the colleges to which he delivered wine, discussing the exploits of the rapist and commiserating with the victims. Every evening he crossed Newmarket Road from his work at Dolamore's, and bought a copy of the *Cambridge Evening News* to see what the police were saying and doing with regard to the rapist investigation. Towards the end, the front door of Dolamore's office even carried the "Wanted" poster, issued by the newspaper, displaying the third photofit, and Cook would tut-tut about the "animal" to customers. He even delivered wine to the newspaper's headquarters, for receptions, and would chat amicably with the office girls who worked there.

One major question that was tackled by the *CEN* on October 3rd was: Could Cook have been arrested earlier? As DCS Naan rightly told the paper, "It is easy to be wise after the event. Despite the rumour and gossip, all we had against Cook was his height. You cannot prosecute or even arrest on rumour. The rapist was going to be caught only in the commission of a rape, going to it or coming away from it with his gear. No one would ever have found it. It had been hidden among 2.5 acres of rough country dotted with shacks and tumble-down out-buildings. As it was, we found it on him. We were not dealing with any two-bit tearaway. We were dealing with a cold, callous, cunning, clever criminal who knew he was safe while we had nothing on him. Consider the alternative. If we had had even the flimsiest of evidence, which we hadn't, and we had arrested Cook, it would have meant in December five girls being dragged through the courts giving evidence in a trial which would have had little or no chance of success. They would have suffered twice over for nothing. And the rapist would most likely have gone free."

In fact, Cook had indeed been one of several suspects as early as December 1974 — his name had frequently been suggested by serving policemen and members of the public who had known him since childhood. This was hardly surprising, since the rapist was clearly a short man and an expert house-breaker. Cook was one of 1644 men in the Cambridge area who were 5 ft 5 ins. tall or less, and one of about 100 men in the area with a criminal record. On the other hand, he had never before been involved in any crime involving sex or violence — he was simply a cat burglar. Unfortunately the errors made about his age by the first victims helped to deflect the suspicions: they all said he was twenty or in his twenties (it was only in April 1975 that Gail G. reported that he was in his forties).

It was revealed during the trial that on December 23rd, 1974, Cook went to the police at their request. He said, "I wondered how long it would be before you wanted to see me. I am the right build. But I am 46." He claimed he had an alibi in that he was at home in bed with his wife. He had a copy of the first photofit picture with him, and denied all allegations, knowing the police were powerless without evidence. A search was made at that time of his caravan and out-buildings — all were clean. His wife also supplied an alibi for the times of the rapes and the attacks.

Along with other suspects he was seen again in February 1975, but still nothing linked him to the attacks except his height and his house-breaking expertise. On May 6th, after the lunchtime rape in Pye Terrace, the police had all their suspicions of Cook smashed, because squads had raced to the workplaces of suspects. Cook was found calmly working with his van. He said he had been at Banham's boatyard at the time of the rape, and police found three independent people, including a senior manager, at Banham's who confirmed his alibi in good faith — what they did not realise was that he had slipped away from the boatyard for half an hour to go round the corner to Pye Terrace, wearing a wig, dark glasses and some makeup. He had then returned to the boatyard, hiding his disguise by the river, and had rejoined the unsuspecting men by the time the ambulance went by to pick up his victim. According to the *Daily Mail* of October 4th, Cook returned to the marina later that day and told receptionist Mrs Jillian Rathbone, "The police had no right to question me like that. I know my rights." She said, "He was very cross at first, and then made some joking remarks about being pleased nobody had found his catalogue of rape masks."

Fortunately for Cook, police had another suspect in mind, in the right age and height group, who had connections with the places where the girls were raped, and who had a peculiar saliva grouping. Cook had not taken the saliva test because he was outside the age group, and police had no power to force him or anyone else to take a saliva or blood test. One tabloid claimed that, at the time of his capture, plans were being laid to trick Cook into unwittingly giving a saliva sample, but Bernard Hotson has told me that this is untrue. Another tabloid claimed that he had been the first person who was asked to take a saliva test but had refused — this too was untrue. In any case, even a positive saliva test would only have strengthened suspicions, it would not have proved the case. He never left a fingerprint or anything at all. It was absolutely vital to find his rapist paraphernalia. As Cook himself told DCS Naan, "You'd never have got me without the gear."

Since the saliva tests had started, Cook may have assumed that his turn would come despite his age, and so was perhaps growing desperate, knowing the game was soon to be up — perhaps therefore some part of his subconscious wanted to be caught. The attack on the hostel was reckless in the extreme, and he had very rarely been reckless, with the exception of the attack on Elizabeth C. The building was filled with people, and all its lights were kept on at night. How could he possibly have believed that he could get away with it? Or was he just getting too cocky, believing in his own "legend" and his continuing ability to elude the law because he was simply too old to be under suspicion?

A happy ending

On October 4th, the front page of the *CEN* revealed the recipients of the reward money totalling £1500. It will be recalled that £1000 had been offered by the newspaper for information leading to the arrest and conviction of the rapist, and then two local businessmen each offered a further £250 — Mr C. Ronayne of Damp and Decay Control Ltd, and Mr John Carlin of C and M Plasterers Cambridge Ltd. In consultation with DCS Naan, it was decided to award £300 to 5 individuals. First, of course, was the arresting officer, DC Terry Edwards, but as a serving officer he was not allowed to receive reward money, so accepted it on behalf of the Police Benevolent Fund.

The second recipient was Michael Lawrence, the resident of 48 Selwyn Road who helped DC Edwards to detain Cook. The two night-fishermen who raised the alarm that night after hearing screams at Owlestone Croft — Harry Jeffries and Ray Holland — were also rewarded, while the fifth man was Everall Ballantyne, a member of the portering staff at Addenbrooke's Hospital who had been in bed on the ground floor of the hostel, who dialled 999 a few seconds before Mr Holland, and made a search of the building at some risk to himself.

The Chief Constable of Cambridgeshire, Frederick Drayton Porter, was justifiably proud of his men. He had been proved right in rejecting the front-page plea in the *News of the World* of May 11th for him to call in Scotland Yard. As he had said at the time, the Yard had no specialist dealing with rape as it had for murder. After the trial, he emphasised that "This case has proved the real danger of the pornography which is being commercialised and allowed to go unchecked on the alleged grounds that censorship interferes with the liberty of the individual." He expressed his gratitude to the people of Cambridge, particularly those who were under suspicion because they fitted the descriptions given by the rape victims. He thanked the press, and singled out Fulton Gillespie for particular praise for his responsible reporting from the beginning. He also thanked those under suspicion for volunteering to come forward to assist. It was especially gratifying when he said, "We are sometimes critical of the undergraduates of the university, but in this inquiry their help and assistance, particularly in providing escorts, was invaluable."

But he saved his greatest thanks for his men, and he issued a special congratulatory order to them which read: "Quod Erat Faciendum, Quod Erat Inveniendum, Quod Erat Demonstrandum. I am proud of you all" (Which had to be done was done, Which had to be found was found, Which had to be proved was proved).

Everall Ballantyne   Harry Jeffries   Ray Holland   Michael Lawrence

FIVE SHARE
RAPE HUNT
REWARD

Terry Edwards

The five recipients of the reward and the award ceremony

Chapter 13
The aftermath

One might have thought that, once he had been sentenced to life imprisonment, the strange story of Peter Cook was over. But there were still some very bizarre twists in the tale to come.

It took the law some time to figure out where to put him. He was first kept in the hospital wing of Gartree Prison (Leicester) for a period of assessment, and by November was in Wormwood Scrubs; he would then be transferred to a maximum security prison to serve his sentence — but which one? The three most likely candidates were thought to be Gartree, Parkhurst and Durham. However, if he were to request protection from other prisoners, or if prison authorities felt his presence was disturbing to other prisoners, he could be transferred (under Rule 43 of the Prisons Code) to either Gloucester or Reading Jail, two prisons which catered specially for men who had committed crimes against women and children, especially sex offenders. This kind of criminal is most despised by prison inmates, and their presence can often be a threat to the delicate balance that exists in even the best-run prisons between staff and prisoners.

Rule 43 stated that "Where it appears desirable for the maintenance of good order or discipline, or in his own interests, that a prisoner should not associate with other prisoners, either generally or for particular purposes, the governor may arrange for the prisoner's removal from association accordingly". In 1975, 480 men out of the more than 40,000 in prison had claimed the protection of Rule 43. However, there was a three month waiting list to get into Gloucester; no information was available to the press at the time for Reading. It was certainly likely that Cook would require such protection — Mrs Mildred Cousins, who was his wife's aunt, told the *CEN* that "Margaret has visited him at least once while he was waiting to be tried. She said he told her he could not stand it in jail, being shut up. She told me he had been in hospital because the other prisoners had got at him. I saw one of the pictures of him and he had a big scar on his face. I don't think the other prisoners will leave him alone for long."

In January 1976 it was announced that Cook had been transferred to Parkhurst high security prison on the Isle of Wight. He had been classified as a category "A" prisoner, wearing the uniform of a high-risk prisoner — dark blue tunic and trousers with a bright yellow patch on both. It was revealed that, while at Gartree, he had been placed in the prison's hospital for his own safety with a guard in attendance at all times. He was to be housed in Parkhurst's Special Wing, reserved for particular types of prisoners whom the authorities felt might be at risk.

After the trial, DCS Naan was at last able to enjoy a holiday in Majorca with his wife and two daughters — a holiday he had earlier had to cancel because of the rape hunt. But what of the victims? On October 4th, the *CEN* provided the last details of them which would ever be made known. One of them attended the trial, before being escorted back to her Midlands home by a policeman friend. She was the only one who felt able to face the ordeal; she sat throughout the hearing, pale but composed, and did not leave her seat until the life sentence was passed. Of the other victims, only one had stayed in the Cambridge area. Three were abroad (in Canada, Australia and Africa), and the others were in various parts of England — one in Warwickshire, another in the West Country, and one in Huntingdonshire. "Only one girl has still to recover from her ordeal. She cannot talk about it even to her doctors. She has even hidden the fact that she was a victim from her widowed mother."

The first dramatic turn of events involved Margaret, Cook's wife. Predictably enough, three Sunday newspapers — the *People*, the *Mirror* and the *News of the World* — vied for salacious details of the case on October 5th. The startling headline on the front page of the *People* was: "Dad kicks out rapist's wife". It claimed that Cook's father had told Margaret, "Pack your things and get off my land." He said she should remove the caravan from the bottom of his garden, or he would burn it down. This was only days after Cook had written to her, "Look after my mother and father for me. Offer them help, love and kindness."

The journalist said that he had spoken to Sam behind the drawn curtains of his house, and was told: "I'm giving Margaret notice to get off my land as soon as she likes. I don't care if I never see her again. If she won't go, I shall set fire to her caravan and that'll be the end of it. I have cut Peter out of my will completely but my wife could not bring herself to do the same. She is leaving £3000 for him in trust, although I said she was a bloody fool." He and his wife are filled with bitterness not only for their son but also for Margaret: "As far as I am concerned I have no son. What he did to those girls no one can excuse. He always had money. Why the hell couldn't he have gone into town. There are plenty of whores there." Sam had burned every picture of his son in the family album, and torn up every letter sent from prison. "I thank God the judge asked him to be kept in jail for the rest of his life."

There could be no happy ending for Cook's unfortunate parents, but, as the *CEN* reported on November 13th, they did receive great kindness from friends and strangers alike. At first they had been afraid to cross their doorstep for fear of public reaction; but, as Sam reported, "We needn't have worried. People have been so kind, you wouldn't believe it. We've had letters from all over the country from people we have never met, offering us kind words and comfort... I was honestly frightened to meet [my former business acquaintances] again, but since we have had the letters, I just thought, well, we have got to get on with what's left of our lives. It has given me a new lease of life just to meet these old acquaintances again and discover that they hold nothing against us." Dora, who had been ill for months after her son's arrest, added that, "Our neighbours and the people in the village have really put themselves out not to make us feel uncomfortable. We didn't know what we were going to do when all this happened...We'd just like to say a sincere thank-you to all the local people and to all the people from around the county who have written to us; we discovered we had got friends we didn't know we had."

Inevitably the three Sunday papers in question focused their attention on Cook's sex life with his wife, and on her dilemma as to whether she was partly responsible for his crimes. In the *People*, she was quoted as saying, "If I hadn't resisted my husband's sexual advances so much he might not have been where he is today. The truth is that after I got married I lost interest in sex. It still has no appeal for me. I realise now that a man is different from a woman in that respect. If he can't be satisfied with his wife, he is going to turn elsewhere." As she thumbed through her wedding album, she continued, "My husband was too demanding. Sometimes he wanted sex two or three times a day. But nearly always I turned him down. A wife gets tired. I refused to jump into bed because Peter was feeling sexy." She said that her husband "was not the world's greatest lover", and it had become impossible for him soon after their marriage, to "make love in the proper way. But even so I should have responded to his kisses. Perhaps he could have got the satisfaction he needed if I'd been a bit more responsive." She thought it was an operation he had which affected his sexual activity.

"He became more frustrated and I grew more frigid. Then he came home with a camera and asked me to pose in the nude or wearing sexy nighties. I thought the whole thing was disgusting. I couldn't bring myself to do it. When he bought a projector and started showing dirty films I felt sickened. Whenever we had a film session or when he read out bits from dirty books he would get very sexy and I would just get more frigid."

Margaret was keen for the *People* to highlight the other side of her husband's nature, "so that everyone may know he is not as black as he's painted." She showed them a letter he had written to her from prison three days before being sentenced: it began "My beloved Margaret" and ended "Your ever loving husband, Peter" above dozens of kisses. In it he told his wife how sorry he was for the way things had turned out, and begged her to stay loyal to him, saying (somewhat optimistically) that they would still have a long life together when he came out. He repeated over and over again how much he loved her and that he wanted her to keep the home together until he returned. He also urged her to take good care of their three cats, Whisk, Sam and Snowy, each of which also got four kisses at the end of the letter. The cats were very important to him — indeed Margaret had told the *Daily Mail* of October 4th, "We were happy together. There was nothing better than being at home, Peter watching a crime film on telly with one of our cats on his lap."

The letter read as follows: "Whatever happens Margaret be brave. You will 'cry' a lot. You will 'cry' for me Margaret. It will be so hard because I shall never be able to forget it...I think what if anyone 'raped' you, how I would feel. So, Margaret, we have to share the sorrow... No one knows what is going to happen to me. I don't want you to be unhappy because if you are, think how I will feel... I love you ever so much, but I also love my Mum and Dad... Remember that I don't want to die, but I would have if it had not been for Rev. Peter Cane and the other vicars. When I got caught I was in real pain in my mind... I wanted to do all sorts of things. I was planning to end it all so there would be no trial to save the pain and sorrow for mum and dad."

Finally, Margaret confided in the *People* that she and Cook had tried to adopt a baby — thus confirming what Mrs Breed had told the press earlier. According to Margaret, "Peter desperately wanted a child, but we found that because of his condition it was impossible. We applied to the authorities, but they turned us down because we only lived in a caravan. I think it would have made all the difference to my husband if we had had a child. I still love my husband. I hate what he did to those girls, but I still can't bring myself to leave him. I've written to him saying I'll wait no matter how long he stays in prison. At least I have to give him that much hope."

The *News of the World* likewise had Margaret as their front-page story, under the banner headline "It's all my fault. I deprived him of love. I should have given in every time he wanted me". She told the journalist that she had written to Cook after his arrest and told him not to worry, "that I'd stick by him forever and love him. That it was all my fault that he raped those women." Cook had written back that she should not blame herself, and that the blue films were responsible.

She now added some interesting details to the discussions she had had with her husband about the identity of the rapist. "When police told me they'd caught him and he was the rapist, I cried all day. I just couldn't believe it was the same man. He had never hit me or done anything that the police told me he did to his victims. I would have shopped him if I'd known who he was. Looking back, there were some cruel moments. He used to point out the Photo-fit pictures of the rapist in the papers, and he'd ask me, 'Do you think this fellow looks like me?' I told him, 'No, nothing like you.' The picture was much younger and I didn't think the chin was the same.

Peter Cook's letter to his wife and cats

But he'd then turn around and say, 'You know, I think the rapist looks just the same as I do. Have another look. Don't you see the resemblance?' I thought he was just aping around. I suppose it was his cocky nature. Maybe he was enjoying himself, perhaps it gave him some more kicks, I just don't know."

The details of their love life given to the *News of the World* were even franker than those in the *People*: "When we made love, Peter was usually gentle and nice. I could have done without it a lot of the time and that's where I think things started to go wrong. That and the blue movies. And the fact that he knew he was infertile. You see, he had an accident. After the operation he discovered he couldn't have children. I don't think it was a great shock. We never really worried about it because we had each other." (It should be mentioned at this point that Cook had deceived his wife — he told her that he could not have children because of the injuries in the car crash, but in fact the medical records show that he only had head injuries, and his existing genetic condition was not affected. He also used the car crash to explain away the scars left on his chest by the operation to remove his breasts).

"When he first bought a blue movie, he showed me the film in our caravan. I was shocked and disgusted and told him so. After that he never showed them to me again. But that was also when things began to change. Like most married couples, I suppose our love life grew a bit thin. I always worked quite hard at my job, which is book-binding, and was often tired when I got home. I didn't have the energy to make love whenever Peter wanted it. I suppose we made love once or twice a week, though there were periods when I went without lovemaking for two months. As I said, that didn't worry me. But after the blue films he began changing his sexual habits. He used to be a gentle and good lover. Now he was more persistent and wanted to make love to me three or four times a night. And keep going the whole night through. For me, this was just impossible. A few times he started getting kinky, but I also put a damper on that. That's why I blame myself... There were times when, after he'd been out late, he would try to make love to me, but I'd pretend I was asleep. After a while he'd stop annoying me.

The funny thing is that he never fantasised about sex or chatted to me in a kinky way. Nor would he dress up in women's clothing at home or give me any hint of what he was really like." Oddly, in view of his father's testimony about Cook's total lack of interest in other women, she claimed that "When we went shopping in Cambridge he'd never take his eyes off the young girls and women who were in any way attractive. He would talk about them and point them out, saying how good they looked, but that didn't worry me. I believed him when he said he'd always stick by me. He used to say things like, 'That's a nice bit of stuff'. I would reply that I supposed she was all right. Then he'd walk on and seem to forget about it. He never went out with other girls, and that was important. I knew he'd never leave me. He had always been a quiet, lonely type."

She also, for the first time, revealed how they had met. "I found Peter exciting from the very first day I met him. I was just sixteen, barely out of school. That first night we met we made love, even though he was much older than I was. I think I was out shopping with a girlfriend when we met. Those days he had a motor scooter and he'd ferry me to his mother's house. I've never really been too interested in sex. But as a young girl it was exciting. We've had a lot of fun together. Going away on holidays and on the boat. We were good company for each other. Peter always knew how to fix things well and was a good handyman. He liked sitting at home, watching TV with me and reading. We wouldn't talk much. It was being together that counted.

I've visited him in prison as often as possible. There was always a guard with us while we talked. We kissed each other goodbye on each occasion, and I felt as warmly to him as always. Even so he's still worried about me and frightened that I'll leave him. I've promised him that when he comes out I'll never deny him anything. I will give in to him whenever he wants me. I don't think that's being a martyr. That's just showing love to the only man in your life.....I shall be waiting no matter how long it takes for him to get out. Even if it took the whole of my life. When I took my marriage vows in church I said I would love and cherish him until death. I intend to see those vows through."

Less than two months after Cook's trial, two of his close friends were national front-page news: Jack Dunlop and Nigel Bankford were sex maniacs who committed a series of appalling crimes after being released from Broadmoor as "cured" men. Cook had befriended them there, and later invited both men to his wedding. On November 25th they were sent to jail after a judge said they had shown "the greatest cruelty, sexual perversion, wickedness and evil" that any court would ever hear about. Dunlop was given a life sentence after admitting fifteen charges of indecency, kidnapping, endangering life and wounding, involving boys aged nine to fourteen. Bankford was sentenced to five years for indecent assault, procuring and imprisoning a boy. It is interesting that Dunlop was a leather fetishist and loved boats — one wonders if he influenced Cook in these areas.

It was fairly inevitable, after all the publicity, that some twisted individuals would try to copy Cook, but by an astonishing coincidence the first such individual struck in Hull, my home town. James Burns, a 28-year-old unemployed man, dressed like the Cambridge rapist, and armed with a knife and pairs of tights, attacked the same girl twice in five days. On the first occasion, he climbed a drainpipe into the girl's home at 4 a.m. and crept into her bedroom. The girl, a 22-year-old hospital technician, was terrified, but managed to talk him out of raping her. He apologised and fled; but five days later he returned, this time at 5.30 a.m. She woke as he pulled back the bedclothes, and her screams brought her father and brother to the rescue. Her father, a 46-year-old ex-rugby player tackled Burns and, with his son, pulled down his trousers to prevent him escaping. Burns, described by defending counsel as "a pathetic individual", pleaded guilty to two offences of burglary with intent to rape, and one of burglary, and was jailed for five years in December 1975.

Other copycat prowlers were also at work, according to the *CEN* of March 5th 1976, and jokes in poor taste were also occurring — for example, Oxford University students were reported to have recently abandoned a victim at the roadside with "Rapist" written on his forehead as a joke. Far worse was a copycat rapist who attacked ten women in the bedsit land of West London in 1983, and who was described by police as "another Cambridge rapist." He preyed on pretty bachelor girls who lived alone, slipped into homes through unsecured windows, wore a hood, pounced on victims in their beds, and threatened them with a knife. Clearly, Cook should have had more than just his own victims on his conscience.

Cook the thief, his wife and her lover

A major bombshell occurred in 1978 when the *Sunday People* of October 8th splashed the news on its front page that the "Cambridge rapist pleads to be a woman". Cook had apparently made the request for a sex change to the prison authorities at Parkhurst. No decision had yet been made, but if he was allowed to change sex he would have to be put in a women's prison, and this could cause unrest among his new fellow inmates. It has also been speculated that Cook thought that, as a woman, he would have more chance of winning parole on the grounds that he was no longer a threat to women. Certainly, Terry Edwards tells me that this was the view taken by the police at the time about his motivation — Cook would stop at nothing to get out of prison. Be that as it may, the permission was never given and the operation did not take place.

Can it be coincidence that it was in that same year of 1978 that Margaret, despite all her earlier professions of unending love for her husband, divorced him and reverted to her maiden name of Dickerson? Even more surprising was her choice of new boyfriend — none other than David Thompson, the triple murderer who had been released from Broadmoor and become Cook's closest friend. In June 1982, he was jailed for seven years at Cambridge Crown Court for possessing a shotgun and using it to threaten a man, 33-year-old lorry driver David Parsons, whom he believed was having an affair with Margaret. Parsons told the press, "I never had an affair with Margaret, but David was the sort of man to lose his temper for no reason."

Cook's ex-wife told the *Sunday Mirror* of June 13th 1982, "I seem unlucky with the men in my life" (which is surely a remarkable understatement). "I know people will think of me as strange, falling for two men who behave like monsters, but that's the way things turned out. I love them both in my own way." Thompson, now aged 40, had killed his wife and her parents in 1963 by stabbing and clubbing them with a bayonet and rifle. It was Cook who introduced Thompson to Margaret, while the two men were in Broadmoor. The article claimed that Margaret did not know Thompson had slaughtered his family until the journalist told her — which is very odd since, it will be recalled, Thompson was featured in the press after Cook's trial, and the murders he had committed were mentioned prominently at the time. Surely she must have wondered why he was in Broadmoor?

"She paused for a moment as we talked in the kitchen of her two-bedroom house in Huntingdon, Cambridgeshire. Then she replied, 'I hadn't realised he had killed three people — but I would be lying if I said I was shocked. After being married to a man like Peter, you don't get shocked by anything. Most women's flesh would creep at the thought of making love to two men like that. Well, mine doesn't. David has given me two lovely children — a two-year-old boy and a girl who is four weeks old — and that's one of the reasons I still love him."

Referring to Thompson's jail sentence, she declared "I will wait for him. I want to marry him when he comes out, that's all I know." She also described how their romance was sparked in Broadmoor: "I was introduced to him while I was visiting Peter, who was there after a burglary conviction years before he became the Cambridge rapist. One of the problems with Peter was that we did not have a good sex life. Well, you couldn't say that about David. He was a real romeo."

Nothing more was heard of the Cambridge rapist for years, but in 1995, twenty years into his sentence, there were moves to have him released on parole or moved to an open prison, but pressure from Ann Campbell, then MP for Cambridge, helped to ensure that he remained behind bars. In 1996 he was moved to a low security prison in Doncaster. The curtain finally came down on this tragedy on January 10th 2004 when Peter Samuel Cook died of natural causes in Winchester prison, aged 75. Forgotten by the world, the man who had terrorised a city for eight months, and who had been all over the front pages of the British press in 1975, departed largely unnoticed.

Conclusion

The pint-sized sex fiend who brought terror to bedsitter land.
*(**Daily Mirror**, 4 October 1975)*

Cook's character

As we have seen, there were two markedly different sides to Peter
Samuel Cook: to use a well-worn cliché, he can be seen as a kind of
Jekyll and Hyde. On the one hand, he is remembered as a loving
husband, a man who loved his parents (despite all the suffering he
had brought them throughout his life), and who loved animals. It
will be recalled that Mrs Breed referred to him as a "real
gentleman" and his customers found him unfailingly helpful and
polite. The wife of an old friend of mine in Cambridge told me that
she had run a lodging house years before the rapes, and Cook had
been one of her tenants — she remembered him as very nice, polite
and helpful.

Another aspect of his good side which was rarely mentioned
was his brilliant skill as an artist, wood-carver and architect —
under the naked bulb in his father's old shed, where all his kinky
spoils were hidden, there were also — according to Fulton
Gillespie — "magnificent models of boats carved in wood, an
American pioneer covered-wagon (precision-built to scale with
moving parts) and examples of Greek and Roman reproduction
architecture."

And yet this same man had threatened to kill Mrs Breed, was
described by the owners of the Cambridge sex shop as uncouth and
foul-mouthed, and proved to be a callous, cruel, calculating
monster where the rape victims were concerned. As a *Guardian*

leader of October 4th put it: "Few recent cases have featured crimes as horrible as those committed by the Cambridge rapist...the rapes were cruel, premeditated, bestial acts in which the victims were shown neither mercy nor compassion." He was a little man with an enormous ego who thought he could beat the law and the medical men as well. He had acquired some skill in talking to psychiatrists, and yet eventually they recognised his true character.

For example, Fulton Gillespie quoted one medical report as follows: "These offences were committed by a man in clear consciousness, who showed the utmost care in the selection of his victims, cunning in placing them completely in his power, and a total lack of pity or regard either for their natural terror or for their honour. Infliction of cruelty and terror, rather than the satisfaction of lust, seems to have been the over-riding motive." Another doctor's report said: "The only category he falls into unhesitatingly is that of psychopath. He is cool, callous and calculating. He does not have any jurisdiction over his impulses or wishes. He recognises no boundaries to his activities and there seems to be a pathological absence of guilt or anxiety. His own needs serve the purpose of his existence and whether they are anti-social, immoral, or illegal makes no difference. He is therefore a dangerous man, unrestrained and unencumbered by morality. His emotions are always fictitious. He feels no remorse. In summary, Mr Cook is a dangerous psychopath... he is free from mental illness...and is remarkably free from psycho-neurotic symptoms. He is unreliable and unpredictable, aggressive and devious. He is not susceptible to treatment, but can be dealt with in the confines of the prison system."

The *Daily Mirror* of October 4th 1975 consulted a leading handwriting expert, Frank Hilliger, and showed him one of Cook's letters, but without revealing the writer's identity. If that is indeed true, his analysis was astonishingly accurate: he concluded that Cook was a vain "Peter Pan type" whose imagination was "easily stimulated erotically and on certain occasions his sex drives are fairly strong, if short-lived." He was introverted and self-conscious. "At the same time he experiences strong drives to expand his personality socially by way of boldness and a desire for adventure. Add to this a strong and longstanding desire to be recognised as an important figure, which from childhood has been over-shadowed by a dominating mother." He had childlike characteristics and tended to live in a fantasy world.

One major enigma remains in the case — i.e. the four month gap between the two series of rapes. Some have speculated that he was laying low because of having been interviewed by the police in December 1974 — but since he was still very active, visiting quite a number of houses in that time, the mystery remains. Bernard Hotson tells me that he never explained.

As we have already seen, his vanity and his feelings of superiority over the police led him to taunt them during the 1950s, and he told his wife that the police would not catch the rapist because he was too clever for them. It is therefore somewhat odd that he did not taunt the police in the same way during his eight month reign of terror, as far as is known. The Danish magazine *Rapport* (see below) claimed that he did call the police, after the Homerton rape, and told the police that the rapist was speaking, but they did not believe him; he said they could come round to the telephone box at their convenience, so they could see his initials, and he scratched PSC on the paintwork. However, Bernard Hotson has assured me that no call was ever recorded from the rapist.

> 3rd. November 1965
> Dear Sir,
>   Sorry to have to write
> you a letter from a prison,
> but I am up to my neck in
> trouble.
>   I'm asking you a talk

FROM JAIL . . . *letter to a former boss*

Sample of Cook's handwriting

There is a possibility, however, that one episode did reflect his arrogance: as mentioned earlier, after the rape of April 13th, DS Hotson told the *Daily Mail* that "he is a frightened little bastard. He must operate at night to give himself nerve," — so Cook taunted the police and rose to the challenge by doing the next rape in daylight on May 6th. That would appear to be in character — although the foiled night-time attack of May 4th is hard to fit into that scenario.

Alternatively, one could argue that the daytime rape followed by the attack on the well-lit hostel form a pattern of increasing and uncharacteristic recklessness which may perhaps reflect an (unconscious?) desire to be caught before things went too far and a victim got really badly hurt or killed. It will be recalled that his friend David Thompson told the press that Cook said to him, "'If he is not stopped, he is going to kill someone. Someone must stop him before he goes too far.' I realise now that he was talking about himself."

Certainly the violence of his attacks was increasing, culminating in the slashing of Jane Sproul — having started out only mentioning his knife, he had progressed to showing it to his victims, and then to using it. Indeed, Terry Edwards had a lucky escape during his capture of the rapist — Cook told DCS Charles Naan, "I should have stuck him, but he was too quick for me."

Psychiatrists believe that Cook must have realised from 1960 onwards that he was a sexual freak, and this made him less sexually athletic than the average man. His first real taste of sexual relations had been with his wife, and his less-than-average ability in the sex act — as noted not only by his wife but also his victims — coupled with his wife's heavy build may not have been conducive to the kind of experience he desired.

Some have speculated that he sought out good, middle-class girls in vengeance because he desired them but they had spurned him over the years. There do not seem to have been any girlfriends at all before his marriage — certainly none has ever been mentioned. Cook did have an inferiority complex about his height, but the use of surprise, the knife, the outfits and especially the hood gave him new confidence and stature. As we have already seen, the sex itself was a subsidiary and perfunctory matter — it was the humiliation and degrading of his victims which was most important. At least, because he was infertile, there was no chance of pregnancy resulting from any of the attacks — but the girls did not know that.

Bernard Hotson was quoted in the *Guardian* of October 4th as saying that research suggested that very few men over forty commit rape. Moreover, according to data presented in 1984 by Gail Abarbanel, director of the Rape Treatment Centre at Santa Monica Hospital, California, most rapists are not typically crazy, deranged men, stirred up by pornography, alcohol and drugs to satisfy sexual desires. The men tend not to be crazy. They have above average IQs. They function in society. They are loners. If they are in a sexual relationship with someone, they describe it as unsatisfactory in other aspects. They are isolated. They lack empathy. They tend to see women as all-powerful and controlling. Most rapists have sexual partners, either a wife or someone else. While sex is an element in rape, it is not a primary motive. In fact about one third of men are sexually dysfunctional during rape. That people continue to see it as a sexually motivated crime is partly a problem of language, since terms such as sex offenders and sex crimes help perpetuate the myth. Their high comes from releasing this dominance and aggression. The victim of rape is the object of an explosion of aggression and rage. Quoting Nicholas Groth, author of *Men who rape: the psychology of the offender*, she said there were three main categories — the anger rapist, the power rapist, and the sadistic rapist.

Cook clearly fell into the "anger" category, in which rape is "an impulsive, savage attack of uncontrolled physical violence. The offender is often angry or depressed and acts out a desire to get retribution for various perceived wrongs or injustices. More force is used than is necessary to overcome the victim. The act is of short duration, accompanied by abusive language, and the victim usually suffers extensive physical trauma such as broken bones or bruises. The rapist's satisfaction comes from having discharged his hostility. He doesn't do it for an orgasm, he does it to hurt the victim."

Cook and the constabulary

It will be recalled that most of the victims thought that Cook was in his twenties, and this was largely based on his voice since they could never see him properly. It is possible that his voice sounded young because nervous tension made it higher-pitched; but in fact when he said "Guilty" at his trial, his voice was indeed high-pitched. Since, as mentioned above, few men over forty commit rape, this fact plus the girls' mistake about his age helped to protect him — otherwise he would surely have been watched and tailed, as every aspect of him fitted the facts: his height, his expertise at burglary, his strength, his detailed knowledge of Cambridge, and his utter brilliance at getting in and out of places without being caught.

The Cambridgeshire police took a lot of flak during and after the investigation — not least through the *News of the World* proclaiming that they should concede defeat and call in the Yard.

Moreover the *Daily Mirror* and the *Sun* of October 4th claimed that, at one stage in the investigation, a top detective told officers "I do not want to hear the name of Peter Samuel Cook mentioned in connection with this inquiry again. I have personally eliminated him." The fact that these were the only papers to report this makes one have some doubts about its accuracy, and certainly Bernard Hotson denies any knowledge of it.

The Cambridge student newspaper *Stop Press* was remarkably silent during the reign of terror. On page 1 of January 25th it finally ran a story with the first photofit. The story again made the front page on April 19th after the rapes resumed: "Rapist danger returns?" Due to examinations and so forth, there were no issues of the paper between May 3rd and June 7th. But in the next issue, No. 44, on October 11th, there was an astonishing and classic example of "being wise after the event" in an article by Lewis Bronze entitled "What went wrong" which criticised the police as follows: "The methods the police used to try to catch the rapist concentrated more on extra patrolling and vigilance than traditional detection. They seemed to expect the rapist to walk into their hands, merely because Cambridge was swamped with police patrols. So the police were indirectly wanting the rapist to strike before they expected to capture him, which is what eventually happened. But this apparent success does not vindicate their methods. It is possible that some more positive thinking and imagination on the part of the police would have caught the rapist sooner. For instance, the case fits into the classic patterns described by the Institute of Criminology in West Road — the police would have been wiser to rely on information readily available at that Institute, instead of on what must have been unreliable statements from understandably confused and bewildered victims. The attitude taken towards the blood tests was also negative — they aimed to eliminate people, rather than find one. Had they tested, say, "The fifty most likely people", again, they might have found the person they were looking for much sooner."

Such unfounded armchair criticism and perfect-hindsight must have irritated the police enormously. It will be recalled that DCS Naan had already explained to the *Daily Mail* (October 4th) the very sound reasons why the rapist had to be caught red-handed, and why this inevitably meant that the girls of bedsitland had to be used as bait: "So our bait became every girl in Cambridge. We just had to succeed. Our heads were on the block. We could feel the guillotine coming down. It was a dangerous plan, but we stuck to it. It was the only way we could play this job."

In addition, Bernard Hotson informs me that he was well acquainted with the Institute of Criminology, having been assigned there for a spell some time previously. Moreover, during the course of the police investigations, all kinds of people, from magistrates to student leaders, had been invited to the station where the police explained what they were doing, and asked if the visitors could possibly suggest anything more that might be done. Nobody did so.

In Cambridge, the police investigation had completely changed some aspects of city life for eight months. The crime rate declined significantly through the increased police activity, the spot checks, and detectives dressed to look like students. In particular, burglary declined sharply because of the fear of being caught and then accused of being the rapist. As Terry Edwards has described it to me, the situation created a unique atmosphere in the city, and somehow brought people together — everyone understood what a difficult task was facing the police and was happy to help. Cambridge has never experienced anything of the kind since then.

Fulton Gillespie in the *CEN* of June 9th listed the historical features of the case: "The Cambridge rape hunt is making British criminal history as a police operation without precedent. It has involved more men than many murder inquiries and employed the most sophisticated electronic detection aids — devices never before used in any criminal investigation. Police have had 300 men working in shifts of 100 at a time, staking out every inch of the city's sprawling bedsit land. The inquiry has been going on for eight months and the man in overall charge, DCS Charles Naan, the CID chief of Cambridgeshire police, has tried various ploys to bring to an end the series of rapes and attacks. Although DCS Naan is the man in overall charge of the enquiry, the man leading the hunt on the ground is DS Bernard Hotson, his deputy, and the father of a 22-year-old girl. Both he and his boss and their 300 men have been putting in sixteen and eighteen hour days since the inquiry started. They have each tried to get one rest day every four weeks, but even that has not always been possible. Both CID chiefs cancelled their holidays and on several days have had no sleep at all.

At Parkside police headquarters the operational base for the rape hunt, the offices on the first floor were vacated by their regular occupants and taken over by the rape squad. Thousands of cards in a cross-check index file have kept the hunters up-to-date on who has been seen, where, when and with what result. Masses of forms detailing men who volunteered for the now-famous saliva test have been going into tall grey filing cabinets for ready reference, and rows of daily log books detail all calls both in person and by phone that have come into the rape incident room. The saliva tests have led to a massive forensic examination exercise on swabs taken from the girls, and meticulous searches of all the rooms where the rapist struck. Police have brought in dozens of pairs of night-binoculars and a vast array of sophisticated electronic gadgetry with which they have bugged and sensitised houses in chosen areas of bedsit land." According to Bernard Hotson, these bugging devices, which were very crude by today's standards, were installed in a number of all-girl houses in areas such as Victoria Road which seemed to be likely targets for the rapist. It was a hit-and-miss strategy, in view of the huge odds against managing to bug the very house he would attack next, but at least it gave the girls in question some peace of mind.

The main police team, headed by Naan and Hotson

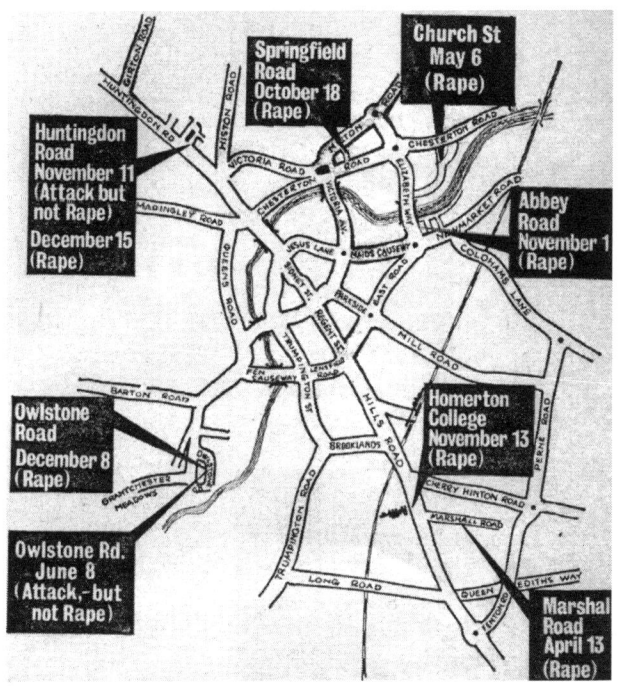

Map of Cambridge showing where the Rapist struck

The *CEN* of October 3rd gave the statistics of the case. After the Pye Terrace rape on May 6th, every available policeman in Cambridge had been mobilised in the effort to catch the criminal. By the end, 500 men and women of all ranks were involved, and the operation cost a total of more than £250,000, a huge sum at that time. No less than 40,000 man hours were spent on the inquiry; 10,000 bedsitters in a 7.5 square mile area were policed; 15,000 phone calls were handled; 30,000 card index references to suspects were filed; 3482 statements were written down by detectives; 2510 positive inquiries were followed up; 1644 saliva tests were carried out; and 400 letters with information were received and answered.

Despite the press criticism, it is very hard to see how the police could have done anything more, or anything differently, at that time, given the very few clues which Cook was leaving, and the mistakes made by the victims about his age. One should be grateful that circumstances — and quite a lot of luck — led to Cook's capture, red-handed. In the words of DCS Naan, "He was a worthy adversary — he led us a right old dance. But we have had the last laugh, haven't we?"

Could it happen again?

This amazing case had a number of utterly unique aspects: the reign of terror itself; DS Hotson's groundbreaking recommendation that boyfriends should be allowed to stay the night; the student bodyguard service; and the saliva tests. But its circumstances were very much of its time, the mid-1970s. There were no CCTV cameras on which Cook might have been glimpsed coming or going; the police had to work with index cards, not computers; there were no DNA tests or records — such profiling was more than ten years away; and above all, there were no mobile phones — and so, because he cut the phone lines, girls had to either wake their neighbours or find a local telephone box which had not been vandalised. Thanks to mobile phones, no victim could be cut off from the world in that way again; hence, for that reason alone, modern technology has ensured that nothing like Cook's campaign could happen today.

The extreme gravity of what the Cambridge rapist managed to do during those eight months explains why the judge at his trial recommended that the life sentences should mean life — this was highly unusual for a crime other than murder, and it was met with some criticism at the time, However, a leader in the *CEN* of October 6th explained why the city approved this outcome for the man whom DS Hotson had described as Cambridge's "vicious shadow": "During all those long dark months, Cambridge suffered in a way unknown to a quiet city. Girls were constantly fearful and so were the families and friends, and young men felt the pressure of suspicious stares and jokes. For the last fifty weeks the 'Beast of Bedsit Land' has dominated many conversations in Cambridge. It is all over now, although the victims can never forget. Peter Cook is beginning his life sentence; some well-minded people may be horrified, as the judge at Norwich forecast they would be, by his observation that life should mean life, but there are very few people here who will share that emotion. In Cambridge, the horror is not beginning, it is over."

Postscript

In March 1976, Cambridge University's Department of Archaeology organised a fieldtrip to see the antiquities of Denmark, and I was one of the students who went along on this interesting and enjoyable jaunt. Passing a newsagent in Copenhagen one day, I suddenly spotted a magazine cover which featured a small photo of a leather mask with "rapist" written in white on it. I therefore bought the magazine (*Rapport*), and discovered something extraordinary — it was starting to serialise the story of the Cambridge rapist, but presented as if written by Cook himself, together with the testimony of all the victims. Even more extraordinary was the fact that each attack was illustrated with a whole series of salacious "reconstruction photographs" featuring beautiful and shapely young girls and a young bearded man. The whole thing was tasteless in many ways, but proved invaluable in that these were the fullest and most detailed versions of the victims' statements to the police which have ever been published, albeit in Danish. The saga spanned four issues of the magazine, but it was only the first one which carried a tell-tale photo on the cover — in other words, had I been in Copenhagen in any other week I would never have learned of the existence of the magazine and its series. Such is the fickle finger of fate, and this episode makes me sure that it was my destiny to produce a book about this astonishing story.

In preparing this account, I have drawn primarily on the newspaper reports of the time, as well as on my diaries, my memory and the memories of friends. There have been very few publications devoted to the case (they are listed below); but by an amazing coincidence, just as my writing was coming to an end, I learned that in 2010 a television documentary about the case had been made by the Twofour Group. This programme, entitled "*The Cambridge Rapist*", proved to be an excellent and well-researched piece of work, produced, directed and filmed by Stuart Pender. It contains some acted reconstructions, complete with dramatic music, but nothing salacious; and Bernard Hotson features prominently throughout, along with other people including a brief appearance by Richard Jopling.

Finally, I had always assumed that the rapist's infamous gear, and especially his iconic mask, had been preserved in a local version of Scotland Yard's "Black Museum", but was astonished to be told by Bernard Hotson that the material was all destroyed years ago — Charles Naan had decided to get rid of it. Only photographs survive. So Cook has gone, and so have the tools of his trade. All that remains of the "Beast of Bedsitland" is the extraordinary story of his life and his terrible deeds.

"The Cambridge Rapist" 1994. in *Real-Life Crimes...and how they were solved* vol. 6, part 77: 1688-95. Midsummer Books: London.

Gillespie, F. 1976. The Cambridge rapist: half man, half woman, complete enigma. *Verdict* vol. 1, No. 2, June: 6-11, 16-19.

Rapport magazine (Copenhagen), Nos 11 to 14, March-April 1976.

Rapport magazine and
photo-reconstruction